Grandpa,
Were You Young Once?

A look at who we were, what we did, what we learned
and how times have changed for our grandkids

WILLIAM C. GOULD

ISBN: 1468089706
ISBN 13: 9781468089707

Table of Contents

SECTION ONE: CHILDHOOD MEMORIES

Grandpa, when you were young, which were your favorite . . .

SECTION TWO: SCHOOL DAYS

Grandpa, when you were growing up . . .

SECTION THREE: GOOD OLD DAYS

Grandpa, now that you're older tell me about . . .

Getting the Most Out of This Book

Winston Churchill said, "The further you can look back, the farther you can see ahead."

This book is not a one night read, but rather is meant to be a *tour companion that inspires and helps a senior reader revisit his or her own special memories,* one subject at a time. When done reminiscing about the first subject, the reader can move on to the next of twenty-six interesting, memorable side roads along the familiar highways that we traveled during our lives. The stories in this book are ones I personally recall, plus some that were suggested by others. Of course, the reader's memories will vary from these stories, based on where they grew up, their family history, and serendipity, but the magic of personal memories has a special place in everyone's heart.

Most seniors are amazed at how much they can remember. A few say they have no old memories. But a few words and examples usually make the memories come flooding back. Then, as they rediscover their unique "good old days," they also recall how much our generation accomplished and how many personal "lessons of life" still apply today. This is a feel-good book, but offers some interesting insights about where we have been, where are today, and what all that might mean to our grandkids. In other words, the book is designed to be fun, but also to help readers understand and feel more secure about the huge changes that have happened in the course of our lifetime.

Despite my seventy years of memories, I learned even more about the "good old days" while leading seminars at a variety of senior centers. My original goal was to help seniors create a Memories booklet for the family—a small book that used the power of storytelling by highlighting a senior's special moments and lessons they had learned. This book builds on that seminar experience, provides a fun way to revisit those old memories, and shows one way of organizing, recording, and treasuring those special moments.

In the seminars (and in the book), I would ask a question, much as a grandchild might, about a topic of personal memories—such as school days or first dates—and ask the audience members to tell the stories that they personally associated with that subject. Immediately, you could see that a grandchild's question triggered a flood of unique thoughts, memories that folks did not realize were still stuck in the corners of their minds. I was amazed! In my many decades of presentations on other subjects, I have never had the audience get so involved, provide so many smiles, or contribute so many special comments; their memories were a joyful experience. In that same vein, this book is not designed as a history book about specific dates and huge events. The book is about the little things that make a life a life. The unique "little things" are what provides joy to the most readers.

In the book, I provide over two-dozen topics, each one posed as a grandchild's simple question. I chose questions around which many memories seem to cluster. The grandchild's questions that I use in the book are organized in three sections. The questions progress from highlights of childhood to school days and finally discuss more recent memories as adults. Each section has a selection of subjects defining that period—for example, the "Childhood Memories" section has subjects like "Toys" and "Books." Each subject is further divided into time-related views:

- **It Seems Like Only Yesterday**—covers a selection of personal memories stressing special moments in our lives and how those moments shaped the way we grew up (for example, looking at the toys you had as a kid). "Yesterday" is defined as beginning in the '40s.

- **Today and Tomorrow**—briefly looks at how those golden years influence our lives today, as well as peeks at where tomorrow might lead (e.g., looking at today's toys and comparing them with what tomorrow's toys might look like.)

Each topic has a few blank places where readers can write in their own memories, and in the back of the book they can add entirely new topics. As anyone who has done genealogy and/or wished they knew more about their ancestors will tell you, writing in these personal notes will be a valuable gift to future generations.

If the reader wants to enjoy even more memory "joggers," there is a list of websites in the appendix where they can go online and see a collection of old toys, cars, movies, music, events, and more. They can also hear a Hopalong Cassidy radio show, see Burma Shave signs, revisit cars they owned, and recall old celebrities. Enjoy!

Introduction

"Grandpa, were you ever young like me? Did you have to eat food you didn't like, study subjects that you hated, or deal with bullies at school? Were you ever so frightened you cried? Did you play sports? Did you have a lot of friends? What was your greatest adventure? What was your favorite home? How did you meet Grandma? Did you like your work? What kind of computer did you use in school? What was your favorite TV program when you were young? How come you never told me all this stuff?"

These questions, ones that any grandchild might ask, can be great motivators to make us think back and reflect on the golden moments, people, challenges, and changes that helped each of us grow into the unique person we are today. When you think about the answers, you will also recall the good and bad lessons we all learned; ones that have often made me say, "If I only knew then what I know now."

I have provided my own answers to many of these questions, but of course my answers are based on my personal experiences and will not necessarily be the same as yours. After all, the beautiful thing about living is that everyone has different experiences and develops their own unique points of view. For that reason, the priority of the book is to inspire you, the reader, to think about your own "good old days," recall old friends, and remember the values that have carried you through the years. The secondary goal is to have you share these "lessons of a lifetime" with your grandchildren, so they don't have to relearn those lessons the hard way.

Today, kids can read in history books and on the Internet about all the big events and all the big heroes of our days. But those histories say little about real life, and nothing at all about the day-to-day struggle of cramming for tests at school, missing a third strike in a big game, getting jilted, saving to buy your first car, dealing with the measles, getting drafted, getting married, or getting your first job. These are personal highlights and feelings; these are the real stories that determined how a lifetime was lived; they are what you mean by "what I know now."

Naturally, a grandchild may respond to an answer that you give by saying, "That's so old-fashioned, Grandpa." But we did not get to be this age by being old-fashioned, and our grandchildren would not be as comfortable as they are if we had really been content with being "old-fashioned." For example, our lifetime of memories covers a period with the greatest progress in the history mankind. In radio, we progressed from crystal sets in the early 1930s, to AM-only console radios with vacuum tubes, to transistor radios with short wave and FM, to small, static-filled, rabbit–eared, black-and-white TVs, to console color sets, to satellite-on-demand life-sized shows projected on high-definition plasma screens. Each of us was a part of that story, and our children and grandchildren are the beneficiaries, a fact they may conveniently overlook.

Just think: during our lifetime, science (and better hygiene) has gotten the upper hand on such deadly sicknesses as cholera, polio, tuberculosis, whooping cough, yellow fever, malaria, and the less dangerous (but almost inevitable) problems of chicken pox, measles, and mumps. They are terrible memories for many of us. These are all diseases our grandchildren rarely worry about, thanks to the efforts of dedicated folks like Jonas Salk.

We also helped the movies progress from grainy, black-and-white, silent films on small screens to "talkies," and then to ever-improving brightness, color, and sound. We created bigger-than-life image projectors with stereophonic sound, and even 3D technology for home and theaters. (Just think what *Shrek* or *Avatar* would have looked like at our old Saturday matinee!)

And look at what we, our generation, inspired with the computer! The new iPad fits in your hand and has more power by far than the computers I used at MIT just 40-some years ago—computers that filled a room the size of a house and required air-conditioning and huge cables. Fifty years ago, when we first began developing computers, communications via Internet and e-mail were not even on the drawing board. Where would our grandkids be without the myriad of new devices that were born in our era?

In transportation, during our lifetime, we went from the two-seat Piper Cub (about $1500) with a top speed of 85 miles per hour, to Boeing's new Dreamliner, which seats about 300 people and cruises at about 600 miles per hour. (By the way, the Dreamliner sells for roughly $180 million per plane if you want one, and it seats about 25 percent of my entire home-town. What a deal!)

However, as we all know from experience, progress is like medicine; they can both solve some problems, but they can also create new problems. Just like some of the medi-cines advertised on TV, "scientific progress" has created some scary "side-effects" that might make a senior question whether all this progress has really led us where we meant to go.

We discussed this topic of "side-effects" in one of the senior seminars that led to this book. We started the session with the question, "Progress—Are We There Yet?" See if you can relate to this "Old Philosopher's" recap of the concerns (side-effects) we discussed:

You say you had a 25¢-a-week allowance when you were a kid, but today your grandchildren need $3 a day for a latte at Starbucks. Is this what bothers you? You say your father ham-mered into your head, "Neither a borrower nor a lender be," but your kids have a mortgage and credit cards that look like our national debt. When you mention your piggy bank, you just get blank stares. Is this what keeps you awake at night? Even worse, you thought movies were about plot and character, but now most movies are just pyrotechnics shows with some sex thrown in. Is this what concerns you? You also recall the rolling-in-the-aisle, family humor of Bob Hope and Red Skelton and now we get the crass humor of Charlie Sheen or Roseanne. Is that what makes you sad? Or do you recall the clear words of songs by Frank Sinatra or Patti Page, but think that today it seems music is all about loud screaming over noisy guitars—to the point that it makes even old Spike Jones sound good? Is that what distresses you? You say your mother taught you to take pride in how you looked, but now baggy pants that fall halfway to the knees and don't even cover rear ends *are considered high style, girls' bare midriffs are the "'in' thing" despite the flab that rolls over their belts—and, to top it off, new chests are given as graduation presents (despite the fact that boys are not supposed to look at girls' chests anymore). Are those some of the things that make you think the world has gone crazy? Is that what's bothering you, friend? Me too.*

There is serious concern but also a lot of fun in those questions. Maybe what is really troubling us is the sixty-four-dollar question, "How did we get here?" Maybe, while we were focused on all the wonderful new gadgets and solutions of our era, our children and grandchildren were missing many of the basic values that we learned and which had made our lives so rich. Most of us had to learn the art of self-reliance. We grew up with the stories of the Depression and we prioritized a stable future over buying "stuff"; we actually saved our money for that rainy day. We valued quiet time and using our imaginations. We at least attempted to live within guidelines of morals, integrity, honesty, and common sense, because our close-knit neighborhoods, home life, and/or religious beliefs helped define and enforce those values. My, how times have changed.

This book, in addition to being fun, can be a tool to help you pass on some of the timeless lessons, values, joys, and sorrows that you learned over a lifetime. You may also add comments to our easy-to-read format, creating a personal perspective on dozens of topics that can eventually be handed down to kids and grandkids, in the hope they won't have to say, "If I had only known then what I now know."

However, my primary goal is to help you replay and enjoy the hundreds of memories stored in the corners of your mind—a personal newsreel or snapshots in time of old friends and events, a legacy that offers the best show in town. Your personal memory show may be better than the old Saturday matinee, because the admission is free, it has a great plot, and the pleasure is priceless. Just bring your own popcorn (or, better yet, a grandchild).

"Return with us now to those thrilling days of yesteryear." Join us in section 1 for the adventures and memories of childhood, school days, and growing up.

SECTION ONE

CHILDHOOD MEMORIES

Organizing memories and comments into Childhood, School Days, and Good Old Days is a bit like herding cats. Memories seem much happier going their own way, laughing at rules and categories. To make the job even harder, it is unclear whether my childhood ever ended, so it is a bit fuzzy where section one begins and ends. However, undaunted, I have tried my best to take a somewhat organized approach to those wonderful memories of "Childhood."

In general, childhood days hold some of the most valuable memories of our lives. As Fred Rogers of *Mr. Rogers' Neighborhood* once said, "Play is often talked about as if it were a relief from serious learning. But for children, play is serious learning. Play is really the work of childhood." Childhood is a time when you are creating the basic you, a creation based on events, stories, friends, and family. It is a time of personal achievements—first steps, first illnesses, first words, first emotions, learning to read, enjoying music, being away from Mother, and so on. It is a time for flights of fancy, filled with fairytale characters, holiday thrills, tooth fairies, Easter eggs, perfect parents, and unlimited dreams.

Childhood was a time when our likes and dislikes were not swayed by dollar signs, sex appeal, ambitions, or the need for diplomacy; our feelings were straight from the heart. If we

1

enjoyed a book, meal, or a piece of music, we enjoyed it for itself, not because it was advertised as a classic (*The Cat In The Hat,* for example). We enjoyed sports more for the sheer exuberance of it than for winning or losing. We enjoyed movies because we laughed or screamed and not because the advertisements or reviews said we should. We also learned creativity by entertaining ourselves, either through the wonders of nature or the power of our two hands. And finally, we learned about being hurt—hurt by family tragedy, disloyal friends, disappointments while playing, or the power of our parents' favorite expression, "No." (Of course, one of the worst disappointments, as everyone remembers, was when the ice cream fell off the cone.)

Think back with me now, way back, to when you were six years old. What were the three most important things to you, a six-year-old? Maybe your top priorities were a Hershey's chocolate bar, the family dog, and Mother's lap. There is no correct list; there is only your answer. Let the stories in this section coax out those unique memories of childhood, memories we all think we just forgot, ones that are hiding in the dusty attic of our mind. Together, we will look back at our childhood love of radio and TV, music, books, toys, clothes, and more. We will trace how each topic has changed over the years and how they might look in the future. In this section, the journey back in time might also help you answer a few of your grandchild's simple questions.

Lewis Carroll once said, "I'd give all the wealth that the years have piled up, to once more be a little child, for one bright summer day." For the next few pages, let's imagine we are young again.

TV SHOWS

Grandpa, what were your favorite TV shows when you were young?

*"Radio is the theater of the mind;
television is the theater of the mindless."*

—Steve Allen

1. IT SEEMS LIKE ONLY YESTERDAY

When I told my grandchildren that as youngsters we had no television, it evoked a sense of pity—a level of pity we might have felt for people from the Dark Ages, a civilization bereft of even basic comforts. Dare I also admit that we suffered from a lack of CDs, DVDs, or surround sound as well? How could we have lived through such deprivation? Are we from another planet?

But the fact is we were lucky. We had a small miracle called the radio. Prior to radio, the only daily entertainment available to our parents had been a book, a newspaper, and a Victrola. These distractions were complemented by an occasional movie or by local gossip, as well as self-entertainment from musical instruments or singing. I suppose that doesn't sound like much fun to our grandkids, but we grew up in an environment where work was more important than fun, and parents scheduled entertainment as they could, not as a priority, which it is today.

By the mid-1930s, we had entered the era of rich radio programming, and radio serials became part of people's daily routine. Kids could not miss the latest secret message from Dick Tracy. Mother had her soaps, and Father had boxing. As there were no devices for home recordings until the 1940s, you either heard the crisis of that day's serial show "broadcast live"—shows like *Pepper Young's Family*, *David Harum*, and *Ma Perkins*—or you tragically missed it, requiring an update from a neighbor. Consequently, the top radio shows dictated their listeners' daily schedules. When *Stella Dallas* went on the air at three p.m., it was time to iron shirts. Kids came home on time for dinner at five so they would be ready for *Captain Midnight's* air adventure or the wonderful laugh of *The Shadow*. And then, at seven thirty, they breathlessly waited for the thundering hoof beats of the great horse Silver and his rider, the Lone Ranger. That might be followed by *I Love a Mystery* or *Duffy's Tavern*, and then the kids went off to bed so that Father would not miss the dulcet tones of a trusted newscaster, such as Gabriel Heatter or Lowell Thomas, at nine.

On Saturday night, the family focused on music from *Your Hit Parade* (originally with Frank Sinatra), the *National Barn Dance*, and the wonderful *Kate Smith Show*. Sundays were family radio nights, which began with Gene Autry's *Melody Ranch*; the *Jack Benny Program*, with his guests Rochester and Phil Harris; or Fred Allen's shows, providing clean, light-hearted comedy. Another Sunday show was the *Quiz Kids*, which gave my mother a good reason to tell us to study harder (making us hate those kids).

Radio had many advantages over today's TV. First of all, the commercials were shorter, less frequent, and neither told you all the medical side effects you could die from nor discussed your private parts. Rather than being resented, as today's commercials are, some radio commercials were memorable, without taking a lot of time—the Lifebuoy Soap's BO horn, the Rinso-White whistle, the exaggerated "Duz Does Everything," or "Wheaties, the Breakfast of Champions." Also, some products' ads were presented by the beloved star of the show—such as Arthur Godfrey introducing Lipton Tea, George Burns touting White Owl Cigars, and the stars of *Lum and Abner* selling Postum cereal—having them make the pitch made it more sincere than an ad. (My sponsor favorites were "Captain Midnight" promoting Ovaltine, along with Tom Mix extolling Ralston cereal.)

But to me, the most important thing about radio was that it let you use your own imagination. In our minds, we created the characters, saw the scenery, and were involved in the action. We saw, in our mind, how hard Gene Autry hit the bad guy, felt the impact of the car crash in *Casey,*

Crime Photographer, ducked as the outlaw's bullets zipped past the Lone Ranger and whipped over our heads, and we tilted hard on our kitchen chairs as we screeched around a sharp corner, helping the Gang Busters capture this week's evil bank robbers

Our imaginations were so good that we could describe in detail the squeaky door used on the show *Inner Sanctum*, make a list of all the stuff in Fibber McGee's closet, or feel the wind whistling by the cockpit as we flew with "Sky King." Personally, I still enjoy being the casting director in my mind and listening to old-time radio on iTunes.

Some of my favorite radio shows had wonderful characters—some very reminiscent of local folks that I knew. There was pompous Throckmorton P. Gildersleeve, originally from the *Fibber McGee and Molly Show*; Mr. Conklin, the bumbling principal on *Our Miss Brooks*; the sharp old-timer Mr. Keen on *Mr. Keen, Tracer of Lost Persons*; Henry Aldrich, dramatizing a typical teenager's problems on the *Aldrich Family*; *Bulldog Drummond*, one of many hard-boiled radio detectives; and *Lorenzo Jones*, the title character of a daily "soap" about impractical dreamers. You may recall the chilling opening lines of one of my late evening favorites: "It is later than you think! This is the witching hour, the time when dogs howl and evil is let loose on a sleeping world." That opening was from the thriller, *Lights Out*, which started in 1935 and aired for 12 years.

Of course, old radio had a number of drawbacks, as well. Some readers may recall waiting for the vacuum tubes in a big console to warm up before reception began, or fiddling with the tuning knob as the reception would drift, or listening to static from a storm (or bad tubes) and fooling with an antenna. You might have even given the console a sharp whack to encourage clearer sound—a skill that impressed everyone.

Eventually, those listening issues were resolved with new technologies, such as transistors in the 1950s that improved broadcast transmission, reception, station drift, and sound clarity. We also progressed from a big console to hand-held transistor radios, as technology got smaller and needed less power; we added FM radio for more stations; and eventually we evolved into stereo. But the most important advance, which occurred in the mid-1940s, was the stations' ability to record their shows for rebroadcast or resale. That breakthrough in radio recording was a boon to some actors. Prior to having recording capability, a daily show such as the *Lone Ranger* had its stars broadcast each episode three times, one for each time zone. Lucrative, but boring.

The other side effect of recording technology was the impact on musicians, who up to that point had played live music for almost every show. The American Federation of Musicians, under James Petrillo, had fought the use of recording, but lost the battle and a lot of jobs around the mid-1940s. They settled for royalties, which simply did not make up for lost jobs.

By 1950, a new electronic miracle was just gaining favor. Black and white TV watching, fueled by Milton Berle and Jack Benny, was changing home life once again. The new "boob tube" was accompanied by some progressive ideas that were mixed blessings, such as Swanson's TV dinners. The impact on family togetherness and eating quality has been the subject of a fierce debate ever since. However, the irresistible push for TV came in 1948-9, when Hopalong Cassidy rode onto the screen and captured the power of children's influence on parents. (Hoppy also sold a ton of cap-guns, shirts, lunchboxes and boots!) Not everyone thought that TV was a great idea, of course. Steve Allen, who worked in both radio and TV, once said, "Radio is the theater of the mind; television is the theater of the mindless." He was voicing the concern that TV no longer required us to use our imaginations as we had with radio and books, and he felt that the change from "entertaining ourselves" to "being entertained" had some long-term impact on thinking and learning. (Was he right?)

By the 60s, despite very small TV screens, some wonderful "living color" events were broadcast on this new medium—boxing, a Miss USA contest, Disney's *Alice in Wonderland,* Richard Nixon's Checkers speech, and the coronation of Queen Elizabeth—all of which seemed to make TV indispensable. Radio was simply no substitute, especially once TVs broadcast in color. For events such as the World Series, the Kentucky Derby, an opera, or a stage play, the visual aspect actually <u>was</u> the story.

In the very early days of TV, around 1948 or so, we had three channels—ABC, NBC, and CBS—and their broadcasting day ended at eleven p.m. The format of some early shows, like *Burns and Allen,* came from vaudeville, and shows like *The Goldbergs, One Man's Family,* and *Groucho Marx* crossed over from radio. We also enjoyed some wonderful, educational, and unforgettable children's shows, like Disney's *Mickey Mouse Club,* the *Howdy-Doody Show,* and *Captain Kangaroo,* to name just three. Also flourishing in this new visual world were sports shows like the *Gillette Cavalcade of Sports* (boxing), the *Roller Derby,* and professional baseball and football. In this case, technology had opened up an entirely new industry full of well-paying jobs and endless opportunity.

However, early TV had its problems as well. You may recall watching the old test pattern, repositioning the rabbit-ears antenna for each station, getting "snow" in the picture on rainy days, squinting at a nine-inch black-and-white screen, or Father crawling up on the roof to fix the big antenna. Now we have a clear picture, but so many stations that it is hard to find what you want! In addition, sadly, TV is no longer "free."

Some say that radio and TV advancements are second in importance only to the printing press. True or not, radio shows had quality (Lux Theater), great music (Bing Crosby), adventure (*The Whistler*) family humor (*Ozzie and Harriet*), unforgettable sponsors (Carter's Little Liver Pills), and great casting directors—you and me.

2. MY FAVORITE RADIO SHOWS

MY LIST	READER'S LIST —ADD YOUR FAVORITES
Westerns	
The Lone Ranger	PALADIN
Gene Autry's Melody Ranch	BRANDED
Hopalong Cassidy	THE RIFLE MAN
Death Valley Days	WYATT EARP
Crime	
The Shadow	
Gangbusters	
Green Hornet	
Big Town	
Sky King	
Mr. District Attorney	
Adventure	
Captain Midnight	WILD WILD WEST
Terry and the Pirates	OUTER LIMITS
Sergeant Preston and King	TWILIGHT ZONE
I Love a Mystery	STAR TREK

GRANDPA, WERE YOU YOUNG ONCE?

Soaps	
Ma Perkins	
Stella Dallas	
One Man's Family	
Lorenzo Jones	
Comedy	
Fibber McGee and Molly	
Jack Benny Show	
Duffy's Tavern	
Lum and Abner	
Sports	
Friday Night Fights	
Cavalcade of Sports	
News	
John Cameron Swayze	
Gabrielle Heatter	
Music	
Your Hit Parade	
Arthur Godfrey's Talent Scouts	
The Kate Smith Show	

3. TODAY AND TOMORROW

Today, we can look back over our lifetime at the phenomenal technical progress and professional fields that we directly or indirectly helped grow. For example, radio required major revolutions in batteries, transistors, speakers, transmission equipment, and even special antennas. In TV, camera technology became portable and offered high resolution; this allowed wonderful live event coverage in high definition. TV screen technology is now close to life-sized, with color clarity beyond description, and transmissions now allow many, many channels with an almost unlimited menu of entertainment options. Underlying all that progress was the incredible breakthrough in size, until we finally got today's gigabyte chips. You used to lug a dozen 45rpm records to a party, and now you have 1,000 songs on a tiny iPod. Dick Tracy and Buck Rogers would be proud.

You would think that all that brilliant scientific innovation would create perfection, but not so. While manufacturers spend billions on devices, the TV industry seems to have put more time, money, and effort into commercials rather than quality programming (at least in my curmudgeonly opinion). You may have noticed that, unlike radio, TV commercials take up about a third of all viewing time. While a great romance or mystery is supposed to keep the viewer sitting on the edge of their seat, today we are asked every three or four minutes to consider irritable bowel syndrome and disgusting wrinkles, or to be reminded that there's a pill for that bloated feeling we often have. Any concept of drama, audience involvement, pleasure, or excitement is utterly destroyed. They solved this by adding more sex, violence, and profanity, as blue content doesn't need a deep plot.

Furthermore, why did we go to all the trouble of expanding from a 10-inch TV to a nearly life-sized, wall-mounted plasma screen, only to transmit these shows to a four-inch screen on a cell phone? Who needs that? Also, given all the technical geniuses in TV-land, couldn't we design the system so advertisements did not raise the volume to ear-shattering levels? If I want to hear about wonder bras, I'll listen; if not, I won't. (God bless the engineer who invented the "mute" button.) And do we really need so many features that the remote control looks like the panel on a Boeing 747? Do engineers get a bonus for putting the most buttons in the smallest space? Finally, who really needs 1,000 TV channels? Is channel surfing a new full-time occupation?

One of the lessons of life is that all good things eventually get carried to excess, and we are there.

Tomorrow, our grandkids will see the violent clash of the entertainment titans. The battle lines are forming around Apple, Google, Microsoft, today's TV makers, Facebook, and the movie industry. This may be a winner-take-all decision, a fight to the death, which leaves few survivors. I suspect that the TV industry, for example, will go the way of our old radio shows—only found on nostalgia channels. The beneficiaries of this war will be our grandchildren, who will have an all-in-one device that offers TV, Internet, telephony, Skype, X-Box, and PC functions. The device will be cell-phone-size, and will project an image onto eyeglasses, rather than a screen.

Future technology will probably allow holographic images (4D), which will transmit small, life-like stage shows in your home. Some shows will be interactive, so a story might have a different ending based on a decision you make. There are still endless new entertainment possibilities, for our grandchildren's future.

Sometime in tomorrow-land, your grandchild, now much older, will complain, "All this stuff is changing so fast that I can't keep up with it! It's beyond me." The day they say that will make many of us feel a lot better.

As for me, I just hope I will still be able to get old-time radio and old TV classics. Despite technology, there is still nothing that compares to radio's *Inner Sanctum*, classic TV moments with Bob Hope and Johnny Carson, or the belly laughs on Rowan and Martin's *Laugh-In*. "You bet your bippy."

B

TOYS

Grandpa what were your favorite toys?

"The simplest toy, one which even the youngest child can operate, is called a grandparent."

—Sam Levenson, author and humorist

1. IT SEEMS LIKE ONLY YESTERDAY

If one thing defines the generation gaps, it is the difference between favorite toys. Comparing the toys arranged under a Christmas tree forty or more years ago to today's jumble of bows and ribbons says a lot about our generation gap, society's progress, and holiday spirits. For one thing, the happy little North Pole elves of our era, with their hammers and saws, have been replaced by new elves with graduate engineering degrees from MIT, who use silicon chips and plastic to build the most complex toys imaginable. And I also assume that there is a new breed of stronger reindeer that can handle the increased load of stuff per household. Also, I can't help wondering if the modern Santa Claus gets a cut on batteries, because today everything he brings, even a simple board game, seems to need at least four of them.

In our generation, money was tight and presents were fewer, non-electric, and a bit more practical. However, nothing then or now compares to the thrill of opening a Christmas, birthday, or other holiday present. It is a contagious childhood joy that has no age or time limit, a feeling that has no equal, and a spirit that makes parents, even those in dire straits, find a way to celebrate the occasion.

Most people can still recall waking early Christmas morning, with an excitement unmatched in later life, grumbling as Mother made them eat some breakfast before opening presents, screaming that each present was "exactly what I always wanted." There they were, a bright red tricycle with a bell on the handlebar, a new Roy Rogers gun and holster, and even new pajamas that grandma must have asked Santa to bring; they certainly weren't in the letter we sent Santa.

Of course there was a different gift-giving attitude in our day, one where children were loved but were not the center of attention. Because for grownups, work and household chores consumed their waking hours, and children were expected to amuse themselves. For example, when we arrived home after school, we got a quick snack and then were told, "Get a toy, go out and play, and be back in time for supper"; a sterner version was, "Go outside. I do not need you underfoot"; and then there was the classic, "Children are to be seen and not heard."

Given that attitude, most of the toys and games we received were part of a subtle plot to encourage playing out of doors, such as cap guns that could only be fired outside, or India rubber balls that required a concrete sidewalk in order to bounce well (and also to avoid breaking a vase and facing angry punishment). We could count on bats and balls and gloves for the same reason. Of course, the thrill of getting a new baseball glove overcame any thought that we were the objects of Machiavellian intentions. Your first glove, just like long pants, was a sign that you were no longer a "little kid"—a milestone of momentous proportions.

One of my favorite toys was my marble collection. I spent hours shooting marbles with playmates, some of whom were quite unhappy losing a game if we played "keepsies." We simply drew a two-foot circle on a flat spot of ground, and then each player put the same amount of marbles in the circle. The goal was to knock the opponents' marbles out of the circle, and so to capture them; or, in another version, to knock the opponents marbles into a shallow hole in the center of the circle. To do that, you used a shooter marble we called a Mib—a larger, usually ornate marble, flicked with the thumb at the smaller targets. Your favorite Mib might have a name like Big Red. If your Mib went into the hole, you lost it to the opponent, a catastrophe that sometimes brought tears, something akin to losing a pet. The game was early training in the art of arguing your point of view, hiding hurt feelings, and yet keeping a friend.

Getting a Flexible Flyer sled for Christmas was every northern boy's dream—a vision of flashing down an icy hill, passing all the other kids (sometimes completely out of control), plowing into a snow bank in order to stop, your homemade wool mittens soaking wet, your fingers and nose numb with cold, your galoshes ruined from being used as brakes. What present could be better?

Well, maybe one thing. There was an indoor toy, a Lionel train set that appeared under the tree one year. That really got me excited. It was the only "powered" toy I can remember, the small black transformer providing enough energy to get the speeding train leaping off the tracks, which in turn got parents leaping out of chairs. This was one toy that endured and even was added to over the years—new oil cars, a coal tender, bridges, and even tunnels. So much fun that even the grown ups wanted to play.

We also built houses and forts with Lincoln Logs, and eventually all sorts of gadgets with our erector sets; both toys were forerunners of today's amazing Legos. We had small armies of lead soldiers and lead cars—all covered, I am sure, with lead paint—that either fought or raced across my bed. In addition to those toys, we also had several indoor games to play so we were not "underfoot" on rainy or snowy days. Some of my favorites were Checkers, Monopoly, and Parcheesi—games that could take hours of our attention. When we were stay-home-from-school sick, usually with chicken pox, mumps, or measles, the combination of the toys, games, and radio shows saved Mother's sanity.

There was no end to the childhood games we invented or modified. Since our street had no traffic, we set up old tin cans as a goal, used an old broomstick for a bat, grabbed an India rubber ball, and played cricket. Even better, we played a game called half-ball, which (as the name implies) used an India rubber ball cut in half and inverted. When you threw the half-ball, it could swoop and swerve, making hits with the broom-handle bat very difficult. A full nine-inning game, one where several kids imitated the stance or pitching style of their favorite big-league ball player, would fill a big part of a Saturday afternoon. At the end of the day, our inventive minds kept us out of Mother's way, and were probably among the best educators that any boy had.

Of course, dealing with daughters was easier for Mother, and brothers naturally resented that. Girls could help Mother cook, learn to sew, play with dolls and tea services, and could generally be clean and quiet. They set a terrible example and an impossibly high standard for their brothers. Even worse, Mother could make them new clothes, and some of their toys were hand-me-downs from Mother's cookware. It was an unholy alliance.

For boys, hand-me-downs were a nasty problem. There seemed to be a parental shortsightedness that caused them to see all toys as having equal value until they wore out. How these otherwise intelligent people did not realize that a sibling's castoff baseball glove, tricycle, or bag of marbles was not the same as having "your own" was simply unbelievable to us. It was bad enough wearing a hand-me-down jacket, but a hand-me-down toy was just too much. However, as you may recall, children did not get a vote on these matters.

The parent's directions to go and entertain ourselves also resulted in some creative toys we made for ourselves. My old slingshot was a Y-shaped lilac branch plus a section of rubber car inner tube, loaded with a marble or pebble; this created an awesome weapon against any tin can or neighborhood army. Also, a sturdy bow could be made from an old oak branch, and arrows from straight branches. These weapons, along with cap guns from Roy Rogers, provided all the basics for a "Cowboys and Indians" adventure, a game that provided endless variations and arguments (and is now politically incorrect).

Several of us received new (street) roller skates one year. They were the latest technology, which used frictionless roller bearings that improved speed, especially downhill. I recall that they forgot to add brakes, and my knees and elbows took a few terrible scrapings. (No, we did not use helmets and pads.) Eventually, the skates turned into something new. I made a "scooter" by snitching a wooden orange crate from the local grocer, nailing it to a board, adding a wooden handle to the top and two steel roller skates to the bottom; I spent hours racing down the nearest hills.

Imagine, there was not an electronic chip, a AAA battery, or an instruction manual for any of these toys or games that I mentioned. How did we survive?

2. MY FAVORITE TOYS

MY LIST	READER'S LIST —ADD YOUR FAVORITES
Games	
Monopoly	
Checkers	
Parcheesi	
Go Fish	
Things I Made	
Orange-crate scooter	
Wooden sailboats	
Slingshots	
Model planes	
Bow and arrows	
Gliders from balsa wood	
Sports	
Baseball glove	
Ted Williams bat	
First baseball shoes	

Mechanical
Lincoln Logs
Lone Ranger cap gun and holsters
Lionel Train set
Flexible Flyer sled
Radio Flyer wagon
Erector set
First bicycle

There is a lot more to marbles than folks think. Take a look at this site at Land of Marbles: http://www.landofmarbles.com/mm5/merchant.mvc? Also, erector sets were precursors to today's Legos: http://en.wikipedia.org/wiki/Erector_Set

3. TODAY AND TOMORROW

Today, as you can see, toys certainly differ from those in our era. Sadly, children can no longer play outdoors without supervision as we did. This places a huge burden on parents to keep kids entertained, while still getting their work and chores done. Entertaining the kids was also a problem for Mother in our day, and when harsh climates forced us indoors, we tried to master games such as checkers, Monopoly, and Battleship. Since most of those games needed opponents, Mother was usually drafted during the week, and Father on the weekend.

But today, electronics have stepped in and either digitized our old games (I did not say improved) or added new games of all kinds that can be played indoors. (Computer games were invented in 1952, moved into arcades in the 1960s, and became small enough for home use in the early 1980s. So, we seniors began that revolution as well.) Today's kids seem addicted to competitive Wii and Xbox games, such as Super

Mario, Pokémon, tennis, bowling, and more. Kids can play many of these computer games alone or with a remote friend; this makes these games a mother's best friend, as the kids are not underfoot. However, these are neither environmentally nor pocketbook friendly, as virtually every toy, just like every home appliance, is battery-powered—a worrisome trend, as we now use 3 billion batteries every year! In addition, too many of the games promote violence, which is a serious mental health concern.

On the other hand, many fun toys are actually much better. In our youth, Mickey Mouse was just a mouse. Mickey and his friends were in cartoons and comics and that was about it. Today, Mickey is in theme parks around the world, has cruise ships sailing the oceans, and Disney stores that sell everything from Mickey Mouse sweatshirts to watches. Last year, an incredible fifteen million people visited the park in California to see either Mickey in person or watch life-like computer animated versions of his new adventures. For kids who are busy with supervised activities and are isolated by other factors, and to their parents as well, the evolution of Mickey is a real boon. Walt Disney, again from our generation, took creativity to new heights.

However, the protective environment in which kids usually live today, and the solitary and technology-driven nature of much of their recreation, raise questions about how play-time these days is affecting kids. I am no expert, but I think I learned a lot about life and people while playing unsupervised at the local ball field, pool hall, and throughout my neighborhood. I can't help but wonder whether the art of creating your own toys and arguing your own opinion is a more valuable building experience than playing with high-tech toys. Will the educational aspects of these toys and games create a new level of intelligence and personal independence or a nation of isolationists? Only time will tell.

Tomorrow, some of this generation's toys—the simple, creative, and personal ones—will still be around and continue to be enjoyed. But, I fear that over-protectionist parental feelings will eliminate many of our old toys.

More importantly, educational toys and games, which are already vastly superior to what we had, but which have barely begun to reach their full potential, will continue to advance. In the years ahead, educational toys will change the method and speed with which we educate young kids. For older kids, the new Internet will allow more interactive video toys and games that connect to larger numbers of playmates, in even more complex game scenarios. This will certainly keep kids busy.

The social implications of powerful toys are open to discussion by experts. Will these toys diminish a child's humanity, which is something usually nourished by personal contact? Will they learn so quickly that they have super IQs but no practicality? Will playing a game of marbles or hide-and-seek bore them? Will they spend all their time with a device instead of a friend? Will Disney World and Mickey Mouse continue to feed childhood dreams?

And what about a mother's "go out and play" comments in the future? Could there be a new playtime solution? Maybe in the place of a live playmate there will be an R2D2 type of robot playmate, a playmate who can push a swing, play catch, and serve as a Wii opponent, while at the same time having the ability to throw a magnetic, protective shield around the child and use a stun gun on strangers. Then we will have come full circle, as mothers will say, "R2D2, take Johnny and his toys outside to play until dinner. I don't need you both underfoot all the time."

C

BOOKS

Grandpa, what were your favorite books when you were young?

"Outside of a dog, a book is a man's best friend. Inside of a dog, it is too dark to read."

—**Groucho Marx**

1. IT SEEMS LIKE ONLY YESTERDAY

My mother told us that a book is much more than paper; it is a companion, a teacher, and a guide to unknown places. A book, she said, "should be treated with respect." Mother considered books to be, along with food, the lifeblood of her children, an important source of our world knowledge, the foundation for many of our values, an influence on our attitudes, and a major source of our entertainment. There were very few nights, when we were small, that she did not read us a story. Today, there are very few nights when I don't read myself a story. There we see a lesson we all learned: tradition dies hard.

The source of books, for most families, was the local free public library, with its downstairs room for children's books (Dick and Jane) and storytelling and the hallowed upstairs rooms for serious books that could only be reached through the rite of passage of getting older. Our local library, helped by local supporters and one of the 1,700 grants provided by philanthropist Andrew Carnegie, was blessed with librarians who had a passion for getting youngsters to read more, helping adults by suggesting selections that fit adults tastes, and generally making reading a real pleasure. Our much-loved children's librarian ran kids' contests, with prizes for the most books read. (The idea of prizes or anything free was a guaranteed motivator for me in that era.)

My parents were another influence on my reading; they enjoyed classics and nature stories, and some of their books are still in my library. Also, my fifth grade teacher, Mrs. Sweeney, was passionate about geography, so naturally I was introduced to *The Travels of Dr. Doolittle* and his imaginative creatures while I was young enough to imagine that people might one day talk with animals. That led to other wonderful children's books, such as *Black Beauty, My Friend Flicka*, and later, *The Last of the Mohicans*. I also thoroughly enjoyed some now politically incorrect books, such as *Uncle Remus* and *Huckleberry Finn,* simply because they provided insight on human nature and how a hero faced the problems he met on his adventures. Then there was *Tarzan of the Jungle,* a book so well written that I could feel the lion's roar and the rumble of the elephant charge, and would thrill at Tarzan's bravery.

I also recall that in the late 1930s and early 1940s, money was in such short supply that even the purchase of a book such as *Ivanhoe,* a top seller in those days, had a hard time making my folks' financial priority list. Nonetheless, the Classic Book and Encyclopedia Britannica salesmen would come to our door with a satchel of samples, a layaway plan, and strong pleas to Mother, detailing how important the classics were to her children's future, their children's future ability to get a good job, or—wonders of wonders—their ability to go to college (every mother's cherished dream). Young boys like myself were minor "book" salesmen as well, selling low-cost magazines such as *Boy's Life, Saturday Evening Post,* and *Popular Mechanics,* but I had a simpler goal than the book and encyclopedia salesmen. My goal was to sell enough magazine subscriptions to win a new Schwinn bicycle, one with a chrome front headlight, leather-fringed handgrips, and a shiny, loud siren—a bike to make me the envy of all my friends. Much as I tried, I never got that Schwinn. However, based on that experience, I found that I enjoyed reading the sample magazines from *Popular Mechanics.*

Much to Mother's chagrin, it was an age when comic books flourished as well. New ones cost a nickel, used ones only a penny, and they could be swapped with friends. Most comics were stories about action heroes, such as Captain Marvel, Superman, the Green Hornet, Red Ryder, and Flash Gordon. A few were humorous, such as *Archie and his Gang,* or *Jiggs and Maggie,* and some were classic satires on current events, such as *Pogo.* For a young boy, comic books were irresistible, and though not long on quality, they certainly guaranteed that we read.

Little did I realize then how important reading would become in my lifetime. Who knew that technical progress would mean that, unlike our forefathers, our world would become so complex that we would have to read a 20-page manual just to set an alarm clock or make a phone call? Could we have forecast that a simple purchase of a clothes washer would require reading a ten-page purchase contract, another ten pages of instructions, and a list of phone numbers in India if I have questions? Who knew that I would end up needing to read hundreds of computer books, when "computer" wasn't even a word back then? And remind me again why I did not take the Evelyn Woods speed-reading class seriously.

In our grandparents' day, books shaped only the lives of the elite. Fortunately, within our lifetime, the ability to create high-quality books in volume, at a reasonable cost, and widely available, has become the foundation of education and progress. Assuming, of course, that folks read the good stuff and not just the comics.

Over the years, I have hunkered down in an old armchair and read *Lost Horizon* several times. I have dog-eared copies of *The Adventures of Sherlock Holmes*, as well as books that range from history to humor to finances. I will always be indebted to the librarians of my youth for planting the book-reading habit in my young mind.

2. MY FAVORITE BOOKS

MY LIST	READER'S LIST —ADD YOUR FAVORITES
Early Stories	
Blue Fairy Book	
Uncle Remus	
Toby Tyler	
Grimm's Fairy Tales	

Nature Stories

Adventures of Dr. Doolittle

Black Beauty

My Friend Flicka

Lassie Come Home

Winnie the Pooh

Bambi

Wind in the Willows

All Creatures Great and Small

Adventure Stories

Robinson Crusoe

Adventures of Robin Hood

Adventures of Tom Sawyer
& Huckleberry Finn

Wizard of Oz

Treasure Island

Tarzan of the Apes

Last of the Mohicans

Moby Dick

20,000 Leagues Under the Sea

Sherlock Holmes stories

King Arthur

Count of Monte Cristo

Ivanhoe

Lost Horizon

Magazines

Boy's Life

Popular Mechanics

Boy Scout Handbook

Comic Books		
Captain America		
Terry and the Pirates		
Dick Tracy		
Flash Gordon		
Archie		

3. TODAY AND TOMORROW

Today, there are roughly a million books published each year. The new publishing technologies have dramatically cut the time and effort of publishing a book; the computer provides some level of grammar and spelling correction that makes even novice writing look good. The ability and the power of Photoshop to create wild and wacky graphics is light-years ahead of even publishing techniques, which we thought were advanced just five years ago!

Despite that literary abundance, the classic books from our era and prior years remain most popular. Whether it's by Steinbeck, Salinger, Asimov, or Tolstoy, a great story is a timeless work of art. Technologies do not guarantee quality or even interest, which is why the old masters are still masters.

However, the times they are a-changing. Already we can download these classics from the Internet and read them on a flat, touch-screen device—in most cases with the larger fonts that are easy on the eyes. In addition to young people, several of my senior friends with a bit of arthritis and weakening eyes have found these devices to be a real blessing. For most folks on trips, it is far easier to carry an "e-reader" than several books. So, change is here.

Sadly, however, and due to these advances in technology, we are losing the local bookstore, and with it the personal satisfaction of browsing the shelves, leafing through an unknown book, bringing it home and kicking back with a cup of coffee. A great part of the joy of reading is the ability of a good narrative to stir your imagination, to make you create a separate world in your mind and live with the characters you invented. Everyone needs to be transplanted into another realm every now and then (perhaps, for example, entering the passage and discovering Shangri-La), to develop or appreciate another point of view, to confirm how others feel about a subject, and to open one's mind to the larger world around us. Reading a good book remains one of life's greatest pleasures.

Tomorrow's online children's books will be downloaded to a 3D iPad, where, in addition to print, it will have animation and will allow the reader some control over the action!

The authors may incorporate 3D clips and graphics of key scenes and characters, making the story come alive in our hands—a combined text and video experience. A simple click and the raven from Edgar Allen Poe will wing across the page, screeching "Nevermore." They may add beautiful graphics of castles as a background for Hamlet or Macbeth, with pictures that would be too expensive for a printed page. Other "book technologies" will let the books speak, translating typed text into speech in tones that carry the proper emotions and nuances; others will allow alternative endings. (What if the Titanic did not sink?) Those features will make today's technologies, the ones our grandchildren think are so "gee whiz," look as outmoded as our simple books now look to them. Tomorrow's reading will be a real adventure.

Despite all that, my preference will still be that old reading style that forced my imagination to expand the author's work and made me feel I was an integral part of the story. But then again, if you grew up with your own vision of what Huck Finn looked like, you understand that neither technology nor Hollywood can top a perfect partnership: a good book, a soft chair, and your imagination.

D

MOVIES

Grandpa, what were your favorite movies when you were young?

"Toto, I've got a feeling we're not in Kansas anymore."

—Dorothy

1. IT SEEMS LIKE ONLY YESTERDAY

One of Hollywood's greatest creations was the Saturday Kids' Matinee at the local theater, a matinee that included a cartoon, RKO News, a movie, and a "cliffhanger" serial. The serial was a fifteen-minute segment of a fifteen-chapter adventure centered on heroes such as Tarzan, Buck Rogers, Zorro, Superman, and the Lone Ranger, and the imminent danger they faced at minute fourteen made you come back the next Saturday. Superman, for example, escaped from the strength-sapping kryptonite just before the meteor hit earth, or by some miracle Tom Mix and his horse Tony survived a fall over a cliff and rounded up the shocked bad guys. Do I still hear the cheers?

What made the matinee such a welcome offering was its ability to give Mom and Dad a quieter Saturday afternoon—a real bargain for only a dime. The matinee was also worry-free, as the kids got some wholesome education, such as good guys always win and wear white hats (Roy Rogers and Gene Autry), bad guys always lose in the end (James Cagney and George Raft), being kind to animals is the best policy (Tarzan and Rin Tin Tin), and there are scary people and things out there (the Wolf Man and Dracula). Many of the movie themes of the era supported patriotism (John Wayne in *Flying Tigers and Fighting Seabees*); they also stressed respect for law and order (*Gangbusters and Saboteurs*), and even praised religion (*The Bells of St. Mary's* and *Boys Town*). I don't think I ever missed a Rin Tin Tin or Lassie movie when I was young. I think those dog-hero movies are a big reason there are so many dog owners today; although none of our dogs ever behaved that well.

Folks today may have different opinions on the value of the themes, but certainly not about their creativity. In spite of the lack of special effects technology or grandiose budgets, the plots of the films and their stars (plus our imaginations) conjured up vivid images of life on Mars, the jungles of darkest Africa, and battles on the Pacific atolls. Also to their credit, old movies did not depend on offensive language, splattered blood, or titillating nudity to cover up the lack of plot, yet we were still deeply involved in the story.

We even watched the news! Beginning in 1931 and continuing through the war years, the RKO-Pathe Newsreel provided a visual update on the highlights of the week. It offered information that built up patriotism and communicated several civilian-oriented defense programs, such as rationing and scrap drives. Even as kids we were riveted by some of the war footage.

Most important to us, Hollywood was creating an entire world of legendary cartoon characters, many of which inhabit Disney World today. From the adventures of Popeye and Olive Oyl, to poor old Elmer Fudd, his nemesis Bugs Bunny, and of course Mickey, Donald, Goofy, and many more, cartoons became an American fixture, and they introduced expressions we kids loved to imitate. One can only wonder how many times the roadrunner escaped the coyote or how many times Tweety bird escaped Sylvester, the cat who exasperatedly said, "Suffering Succotash." No matter, their antics always brought laughs.

There were also a host of horror flicks, such as the *Frankenstein* (featuring the incomparable Boris Karloff), the best ever rendition of *Dracula* (with Bela Lugosi), 1942's *The Wolf Man* (starring Lon Chaney), and the scary flick *The Cat People*, all of which kept us awake at night! There were also science fiction films such as Bella Lugosi's *The Ape Man, Buck Rogers Conquers the Universe*, or the classic *King Kong*. No wonder we carefully checked under our beds and had trouble sleeping on Saturday nights!!

Of course, as we grew older, sports demanded our Saturday hours and we drifted to more "mature" themes that were shown in the evenings. Mature themes back then meant *The Hunchback of Notre Dame* with Charles Laughton, Orson

Welles in *The Third Man,* and Gary Cooper in *High Noon.* The closest thing to today's R-rated movies was the cleavage and innuendo of *The Outlaw* with Jane Russell, or the harsh reality of the gangs in *Asphalt Jungle* in 1950. Up to that time, most in Hollywood believed their mission was to help build better people and a better country through entertainment. A mission that eventually must have been lost on the way to the bank.

But the real movie highlights of our generation were the characters that we enjoyed. Humphrey Bogart and Jimmy Cagney were unforgettable. Their flip comments, nasty sneers, and tough guy swaggers were copied by our local wannabes. Comedies had such never-to-be-duplicated talents as Bob Hope, Red Skelton, and Danny Kaye—comedians that could leave us rolling us in the aisles with clean humor (which seems to be a lost art). Dramatic actors such as Ronald Coleman, Orson Welles, Spencer Tracy, Errol Flynn, Vincent Price, and Jimmy Stewart seemed to effortlessly create wonderful, unforgettable characters time after time. In movie musicals we had Howard Keel and Mario Lanza's wonderful, clear voices as well. Graceful, female character actresses such as Ida Lupino, Ingrid Bergman, Lauren Bacall, and Grace Kelly completed the casts and made the plots and a young man's secret thoughts come alive. It was a wonderful era for moviegoers.

I recall getting a job as a movie usher in the hope of seeing free movies. This gave me a small glimpse of the behind-the-scenes equipment. In those early days, the 35mm film was black and white and pretty fragile, depending how many times it had been played. There was also the problem of grainy pictures, dust getting on the projector lens, and even burnt out bulbs—any one of which made the kids stamp their feet until the walls seemed to shake. Slowly but surely, we witnessed the film technology improving until we had panoramic color, stereophonic sound, and we retired the old tapes in favor of DVDs. Even Bogart got better looking on DVD.

2. MY FAVORITE MOVIES

MY LIST	READER'S LIST —ADD YOUR FAVORITES
Serials	
Tarzan of the Apes	
The Lone Ranger	
Roy Rogers	
Gene Autry	
Cisco Kid	
Zorro	
Flash Gordon	
Superman	
Charlie Chan	
Comedy	
Abbot and Costello	
Pinocchio	
Pale Face	
Scary Stuff	
Cat People	
King Kong	
Frankenstein	
Dracula	
Military	
Sands of Iwo Jima	
Fighting Leathernecks	

Classics		
Yankee Doodle Dandy		
Wizard of Oz		
Bambi		
My Friend Flicka		
The Maltese Falcon		
Angels with Dirty Faces		
Westerns		
Duel in the Sun		
The Virginian		
Yellow Sky		

These links will remind you of the movies backwhen:
   http://www.oldfortyfives.com/thoseoldwesterns.htm
   http://www.youtube.com/watch?v=B1Gt6hPuMaw

Old-timer downloads:
   http://www.bnwmovies.com/genre/comedy

3. TODAY AND TOMORROW

Today, the movie industry seems so enamored with special effects that the characters, plot, and content seem to have taken second place. As proof of that opinion, when critics rate the top 100 films of all time, the winners are films like *Citizen Kane, Casablanca, Gone with the Wind, The Wizard of Oz, The Maltese Falcon, The Third Man*, and *West Side Story*. Films from our era—the 1940s, '50s, and '60s—fill 78 slots on the American Film Institute's list of the top 100 movies of all time. These winning examples had great character actors and actresses, gripping plots, and strong emotions. (Of course, my personal top 100 might include the likes of *Abbott and Costello Meet Frankenstein,* but what do I know.)

While there have been more recent movies that are true classics, such as *The Godfather, Star Wars,* and *Jaws,* the big modern-day winners are in the field of animation. Animated films such as *Shrek, Ratatouille, Toy Story,* and *Up* accomplish much more than our old cartoons did in terms of plot, characters, and appeal. When I compare an old Mickey Mouse cartoon, for which the cartoonist drew each movement of the character by hand, to a contemporary animated film such as *Finding Nemo,* I get a real appreciation for how hard cartooning was in the old days and how far it is has come thanks to the computer. It is one example of a benefit from technology. Hopefully, the animated characters are more manageable than the prima donna stars of yesterday.

There are also many new and wonderful documentary films, which make history and other subjects come alive. Ken Burns, for one, has done some incredible documentaries on war, sports, music, and national parks that take advantage of computer and movie technologies to get riveting results. His documentary *Jazz* has been called the best documentary of all time. His work on the Civil War makes even folks that hate history sit on the edge of their chairs. I hope these documentaries are a forerunner of tomorrow's education tools, as they will vastly improve a students' appetite.

Unfortunately, most of today's movies seem to rely primarily on violence, smut, political statements, and fears, rather than relying on plot, message, or character building. The Saturday matinee is no longer safe entertainment, because no one knows what message the kids will get. Besides, a ten-cent bag of popcorn now costs four dollars!

Tomorrow, I hope we will see some major changes to the industry and to the viewers. Due to the convergence of the computer, Internet, and large-screen TV, one can already have a kid's matinee at home, where a bag of popcorn is nearly free and Mother can have more control over what the kids are seeing. As Internet and computer speeds increase dramatically, movies should become a huge library in the sky completely available on demand to users. The users will have the option of suffering with advertising or opting to be a fee library subscriber. At last, an end to TV advertising! Is this heaven?

With this in mind, some people predict that theaters, in order to survive, will specialize and offer 3D or holographic high-tech screenings, possibly in a dinner theater atmosphere. Others see theaters as becoming entertainment centers for live-streaming performances. This may mean that you will get dinner for about the same price as a coke and popcorn! How could they charge more?

The big question is whether the movies will revert back to a more responsible strategy of setting high standards that people should live by. The other question is whether animated characters and mechanical voice-overs will replace actors completely. In some cases, that might get movie stars to stop taking themselves so seriously.

Walt Disney said, "Movies can and do have a major influence in shaping young lives." Hopefully, tomorrow's movie industry will help build a better world.

CLOTHES

Grandpa, what kind of clothes did you like?

"Sweater, n.: garment worn by child when its mother is feeling chilly."

—Ambrose Bierce

1. IT SEEMS LIKE ONLY YESTERDAY

Boys' clothes are one of life's mysteries, a mystery that you would think would have been solved long ago. After all, boys don't really care about clothes until they grow older, and sometimes not even then. However, there were many forces that kept boys' fashions in a constant state of change. Some were due to the weather in our area, the many events our parents forced us to attend, or even how skilled a mother was at sewing clothes, knitting sweaters, and darning socks.

Unlike today, yesterday's advertising played much less of a role in the selection of boys' clothes, unless you count the Sears catalog as advertising. In addition, we, the "clothees," had little or nothing to say about what we wanted. Most clothes were purchased for Easter, the beginning of school, and Christmas, the purchase being totally determined by Mother, and influenced by Father only when it came to sports clothing. Mother was the judge and jury on what was and wasn't in good taste. Of course, Mother had to wash and hang out to dry our mud-splattered, worn, and wrinkled clothes (no permanent press or Scotch Guard in those days); she also had to patch and mend torn clothes and darn worn socks. So it was clear that Mother had, until I went to high school, total veto power over any crazy clothes ideas I had.

The girls had it a bit easier, as Mother made their blouses, skirts, and dresses using Simplicity patterns and her new-fangled electric sewing machine. Mother was still the authority, but had much more empathy, so she allowed the girls to help pick out the patterns and learn to make their own clothes—a part of her training program that we boys would not need.

Mother certainly did not understand young boys in regard to clothes. What she did know was that when we went to Sunday school and the church, we were going to look our best. Even when young, we knew that fighting Mother and church was a losing proposition. She loved, for example, those cute sailor suits that had short pants, and a navy blouse—the one with the square collar, stripes, and a few stars. She also liked knickers and long socks, an outfit that required garters to hold up the socks. Add a white shirt, tie, Buster Brown shoes, and we looked like a Sears catalog. Fortunately, for us, the knickers fad died in the late 1930s. Then there was the matter of socks. For me, any old socks would do, but the knitting craze of the time was argyle socks; these had diamonds of color, which, of course, had to be on straight. ("Who cares," we asked?) Along with the socks were knit sweaters, which were much more useful in those days since we had no central heating, and home thermostats (if you had one) were set much lower than they are today. While sweaters were very functional, some of the colors and patterns Mother enjoyed did not fit any macho image I had. Neither did the "white duck" long pants, white shirt, tie, and boy's fedora that we were required to wear for a church function or on the Fourth of July. Nonetheless, we survived!

The war years brought many changes to our dress code, because rationing and an attitude of more casual dress became the new standards. We went from overalls to Levis or, for some occasions, chino pants. Loafers and sneakers were the standard footwear, and the T-shirt came into its own. The T-shirt design I remember is the one with wide horizontal stripes, but as far as I recall, nothing had a company logo on the shirt. (I still do not understand why anyone would wear advertising, unless the store paid you to wear it—not the other way around. Can't you just see the advertising manager telling the owners, "Oh yes, folks will pay more for Levis if we print our name across the rear end"? Amazing.)

The rationing "fashion" factor, which some of my friends forget, was the government influence on boys' (and men's) clothing. During the war years, Uncle Sam regulated all clothing, not just the well-known rationing of silk stockings for parachutes or gas for the war effort. Each family received clothing ration books that dictated how much, which materials, and even what selections were available. FDR placed limitations on the amount of cloth allowed in a given design, including the size of the belt loops and the cuffs, to minimize the use of material. The new law banned vests with most men's suits, discouraged double-breasted suits, and banned silk ties. (By the way, the government even promoted a new synthetic fiber made from milk protein in order to reduce the use of cotton fiber. Unfortunately, when it rained, the new fiber smelled like sour milk. Who would have guessed?)

If Uncle Sam had so much influence, I do not see why FDR could not have banned snowsuits that were so cumbersome that first grade teachers spent a considerable part of class time unwrapping us, much as you would a mummy found in ancient Egypt. Sailor suits could have been banned as well, to devote the cloth to real sailors instead of poor defenseless boys who really did not want to be seen by other boys as "cute." I suppose I should have been thankful that the government didn't dictate wearing knickers until we were teens, as knickers used less cloth. What a terrible thought.

The first clothing decision I had any say in was the purchase of a Frank Sinatra jacket, which happened because my mother wanted me to go to a dance and I think she believed that if I got that jacket, maybe I would pay more attention to my singing lessons and turn into another Frankie. (No such luck.) Of course, I also needed things she knew nothing about, such as Converse sneakers for gym, basketball, sandlot football, hiking, and just running around. Amazingly, I did all that with the one style of sneaker. No wonder I wasn't a superstar. My sneakers held me back!

Once I entered junior high school, Mother's dress code rules got easier and I was allowed to wear the "in things": bell-bottom dungarees, team jackets, and eventually even blue suede shoes. However, Mother still picked out the white shirts and ties, as well as trousers and sweaters. She stuck to her style guns, following Coco Chanel's great philosophy, "Dress shabbily and they will remember your clothes; dress impeccably and they will remember the man (or woman)." Where is Coco now that we need her?

2. MY FAVORITE CLOTHES

MY LIST	READER'S LIST —ADD YOUR FAVORITES
Short pants	
Snowsuits	
Sailor suits	
Shirt and tie	
Galoshes	
Knickers	
Bib overalls	
Buster Brown shoes	
Growing Up	
First long pants	
White duck trousers	
Argyle socks (home made)	
Long johns with trap doors	
Skull caps and beanies	
Knit sweaters	

Later On		
Converse sneakers		
Team jackets		
Straight leg Levis with cuffs		
Frank Sinatra jacket		
Blue suede shoes		
Peg pants		

3. TODAY AND TOMORROW

Today, due to my mother's emphasis on good taste, I suppose I have a warped mind. Mother's unwritten code was to take pride in your appearance, so that probably disqualifies me from discussing today's clothes. However, I am puzzled about why someone would buy new clothes that look like they have already been worn—Levis with torn knees, for example. If I had torn my Levis, I was sure to get a sound talking-to by a parent; so obviously my folks did not know style when they saw it. My parents also insisted we stand up straight, pull in our tummies, and do some exercise. We would be outcasts today, because none of our pants would slide down on our hips, exposing our jellyroll midriff or more. Even worse, today's shapeless, short pants that come down to mid-calf make hobos from our era look neat by contrast. Today, if I go to a cocktail party in slacks and a sports coat, I feel like I am wearing a tuxedo to a barbecue; it seems that even chinos are overdressing. Amazing! But, what can we expect from people who wear their hats backwards?

Tomorrow's clothes, we can say with certainty, will change again, maybe reverting back to Nehru jackets or progressing to designs from Star Wars. The big change will be in materials. Cloth made from new nanotechnology fibers will produce clothing that is much stronger and more useful, probably wrinkle-free. In fact, there is discussion that the new fabrics will mold to your form (OMG), never wear out, and may even self-repair. Maybe you will step into a shower, clothes and all, get blow-dried and be on your way out; a car wash for clothes, so to speak. Even more exciting, some creative inventor will think outside the box and come up with one type of sneaker that fits all activities! Imagine that!

Of course, if we are lucky, ties will return to fashion, and I can use all the ones that I still have in my closet. Whatever new fashion comes to pass, I hope it is soon, because my double-breasted, pinstriped suits seem to get too many stares these days.

FOOD

When you were young, what were your favorite foods, Grandpa?

"Vegetables are a must on a diet. I suggest carrot cake, zucchini bread, and pumpkin pie."

—Jim Davis (creator of "Garfield")

1. IT SEEMS LIKE ONLY YESTERDAY

One of my first favorite foods was "ice"—imagine that! We local "hooligans" would wait until the iceman would come with his wagon. Then, with his rubber vest and tongs, he would cut an ice block to size and lug a twenty-pound block into the ice chest in our back hall. We would be hiding nearby, and would sneak over to his truck and snitch the ice chips he left behind. Of course, he would never use the small chips anyway, but the supposed danger of being "caught" seemed to give the clear crystal ice a very special flavor, one only known to daylight bandits.

Until refrigerators became more affordable and available after the war, the small home ice chest and the ice man were vital, as they were the only way to keep food from spoiling; food preservatives were still mostly in the future. So ice was a treat, and it saved us from a not-so-gourmet diet of canned goods, such as Spam, codfish cakes, deviled ham, and Swanson's canned chicken. Deviled ham—I still cringe at the thought!

When we finally got a new-fangled refrigerator, we appreciated that we no longer had the chore of emptying the pails of water after the ice melted, and we enjoyed the aluminum ice cube trays. However, we hated the frequent defrosting of the refrigerator's ice-covered coils. It sounds funny now, but the humble refrigerator was one of the great technological improvements of our era. Without ice and refrigerators, mothers were forced to do grocery shopping each day, and milk and beer were served at room temperature (much like Europe). Of course, before modern refrigerators, there would have been no leftovers, either. Hmmmm.

In addition, the local food stores had a huge impact on what we ate. The lack of food preservatives meant that you ate canned foods or foods that were in season, so in winter you ate root foods such as Hubbard squash, turnips, parsnips, potatoes, and carrots. Root foods, left in a cool area such as a "root cellar," would last most of the winter—an important fact because, without refrigerated trucks and lacking preservatives, very few out-of-season fruits or fresh vegetables were on the grocer's shelf. Rather, our winter diet included creamed corn, green peas, lima beans, string beans, peaches, pears, and lots of applesauce, all from a can or jar. And in summer the grocer carried foods such as eggs, meat, and vegetables from nearby farms, thereby reducing spoilage, which is a drain on store profit and a source of angry mothers.

Of course fresh milk, buttermilk, and sour cream (staples at our house) were not grocery store items, but were delivered every other day to our back porch about five in the morning by Cherry Valley Dairy (in wonderful glass bottles with a picture of cows on them). The early morning rattle of the glass bottles in the milkman's wire carrier was a dependable alarm clock for my father. In winter, if no one remembered to bring the newly delivered milk in from outside, the cream of the milk would freeze, popping off the lid and letting the cream expand into what looked like the shape and size of a skinned banana. Cream, before the days of homogenized milk, was used in coffee, and the rest was shaken well and poured over cereal. Ahhh! Even today, I appreciate the rich, full taste of fresh, creamy milk.

The same milkman who came to our house also delivered small one-pint milk bottles to our classroom, the small glass bottles sitting on the floor, warming until noon lunch break when they accompanied our home-made bologna, liverwurst, or peanut butter and jelly sandwiches on white bread and wrapped in wax paper. The sandwiches were a bit mushy, as I recall, but the chocolate milk turned it all into a picnic.

Mostly what Mother got at the grocery were basics, such as a twenty-five-pound bag of Gold Medal flour for breads and cakes, Rumford baking powder, Karo syrup for sweetening, and tubs of Crisco for frying. Mother also preserved fruits and tomatoes and made her own jams and jellies, creating the need for Certo, mason jars, sealing wax, and cheesecloth, things in small demand today. She also made her own root beer and sarsaparilla soft drinks, which tasted far better than Royal Crown Cola or Moxie, both of which cost a whole nickel.

Meats were purchased across the street from the grocery store at the butcher shop, a small store with a large cold storage closet that held an array of carcasses—which meant, unlike today, we knew where our meat really came from. Mother was very specific on the cuts, costs, and leanness of her meat. This was especially true of hamburger meat, as a big hamburger patty soon became a small one if the fat content was too high, and stew meats, which if poorly chosen were too tough to chew. She seemed to assume that a butcher could not be trusted and needed her personal audit of each of his offerings. I'm sure she would be quite unhappy with today's precut meat selections; one side hidden by the package, the size determined by the butcher, and the meat deceptively colored. I imagine we would be vegetarians.

The other thing that determined which foods I liked was our home's kitchen, with its big black Glenwood gas stove and oven, the great cast iron pots and pans, the ever boiling kettle of water, and the tantalizing smells that wafted through the entire house. A beef stew that simmered all day or fresh bread cooking in the oven was enough to bring us home from any pastime.

I would be remiss not to mention the fact that whatever Mother served was what we ate, or else we went without. As we were informed, "She was not a short-order cook." When we rebelled and did not eat something, we were reminded that there were starving kids in China and so we must have a clean plate. No clean plate, no dessert. That was a rule she never broke. In addition, I only recall going "out to dinner" with my family on a few special occasions, such as a wedding. Eating out was considered an insult to Mother's cooking, and a waste of money. However, a hot fudge sundae, now that was a different matter.

Sunday dinners were a family affair where Grandma usually took charge; I suppose to give Mother a day of rest. When Grandma cooked, it seemed that all her children and even long lost relatives showed up. I loved her mouth-watering mashed potatoes and gravy, candied yams, and a slab of smoked ham or pot roast. We looked forward to the grand finale: a scrumptious chocolate cake or lemon meringue pie. Yes, those were the days of favorite foods, Sunday afternoon naps, no calorie counting and family togetherness.

2. MY FAVORITE FOODS

MY LIST	READER'S LIST —ADD YOUR FAVORITES
Wheaties	
Shredded Wheat	
Meat loaf	
Smoked ham shoulder	
Pork chops	
Mashed potatoes and gravy	
French fries	

Spaghetti

Corn chowder

Scalloped potatoes

Fricasseed chicken

Yams

Corn on the cob

Buttermilk

Chocolate cake

Brownies

Peanut butter

Homemade bread

Corn bread

Root beer floats

Pistachio ice cream

Fried baloney

Hot dogs

Plum pudding

Calves liver

Big sour pickles

3. TODAY AND TOMORROW

Today, many of the items on my favorites list above are on the "banned" lists of today's cooks! They are either high in fats, high in sugar, high in starch, or all three—items that are likely to shorten your life or promote all kinds of illness. These scientific warnings seem to take all the pleasure out of eating, making each bite a guilt trip. Far be it for me to question science, but after all those years of such unthinkable eating habits, how have I lived this long? Maybe it was the ice.

On the other hand, the lifestyle differences across the decades makes it impossible to compare what what we ate then and what we eat now; it is like comparing apples and oranges. For example, we walked everywhere we went, played outdoors all afternoon, climbed trees, and almost never sat still—exercise that created a roaring fire for burning calories. Also, our foods were fresh, contained no preservatives or dyes, and were nutrient-rich, a generational difference that is still not fully understood, despite all our science. But an even more important difference may be the fact there were zero fast-food restaurants in our town, no funds for between-meal snacks, and even more importantly, we rarely drank sodas—a drink that many feel reduces efficient calorie usage.

On the other hand, maybe it was the seasoning in Mother's good cooking. No one really knows. Maybe all we have learned for sure is that the human body can tolerate a lot of abuse from its owner.

Tomorrow, we can be sure that food will be different again. The world is supposed to grow to a population of nearly 8 billion people by 2025, a huge increase at a time when we are already having trouble feeding and providing water for everyone. In addition, transportation and fertilizer costs are going up dramatically, so the grocery bills may become very painful. How our grandchildren, who enjoy such abundance, will adapt to a world of shortages and high prices is anyone's guess. Maybe they will invent new ways to pay the bills.

However, there is hope. For, as our generation proved conclusively, people can have much less than what is considered necessary and still live happy and healthy lives. Of course, that assumes there will always be peanut butter and jelly sandwiches; otherwise, all bets are off.

C

HOBBIES

Grandpa, what were your favorite hobbies when you were young?

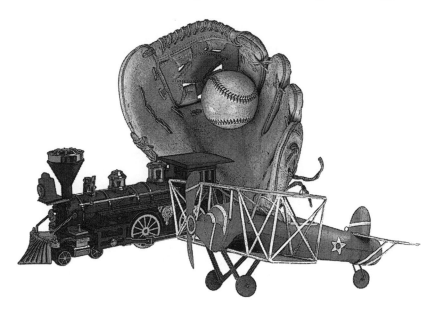

"If at first you don't succeed at skydiving, it may not be the hobby for you."

—Unknown

1. IT SEEMS LIKE ONLY YESTERDAY

As we got older, toys lost their charm, so hobbies were another of Mother's way to keep us busy on rainy or snowy days, although she probably never thought of it in those terms. But three kids running around the house on stormy days, without TV, Wii, or even stories on a cassette tape to distract them, had to call for desperate measures.

During the war years she got help from the president, FDR, who was an avid stamp collector. This inspired us young'uns to order elaborate stamp albums that had clever ways to attach stamps without disfiguring them, plus bags of loose stamps that might or might not contain one we were missing. The US stamps told stories about events, people, and historical places, thus adding to our education, while the foreign stamps provided pictures of exotic, far-off lands that we dreamed about but really never expected to see. Several neighborhood friends were collectors, as were some grownups, so when we ordered a new bag of stamps, it led to a lot of horse-trading. The great hope, of course, was to find one of those rare stamps, one that the government had printed upside down, sideways, or with some other flaw that would instantly make us rich—a hope that had odds similar to winning the lottery today. While that jackpot never happened for me, I am sure Mother felt she had gotten her reward from the hundreds of quiet hours that the hobby provided.

In addition, collecting baseball cards, the ones found in Topps bubble gum packages, was also a neighborhood favorite. This hobby relied on swapping cards with friends and enjoying intense competition. The art of swapping came down to negotiating whether one Ted Williams card was worth two or three Yogi Berras, or whether a Stan Musial had an equal value to a Bob Feller, somewhat influenced by how well a player was doing that particular year and whether he was a local favorite. The baseball card competition came about in a game called "closies," where you slid a card across the sidewalk and the winner was the closest to the wall in front of our house. Players applied advanced technology to make their cards slide better. A technology known as melted candle wax was smeared on both sides of the cards. One play-mate even added a paper clip to make his card slide better, but this was unanimously outlawed, as it was an unnatural advantage—demonstrating, I guess, that democracy really does work, even at a young age.

During the war years, the progress of aviation inspired my hobby of building model airplanes, another self-entertainment activity that took many quiet hours and was relatively low in cost. Model planes attracted many kids because flying, to a young person, was a miraculous adventure that freed man from earth and would lead someday to the intergalactic world of Buck Rogers. The early civilian planes such as the Piper Cub or Beechcraft came in miniature kits; the kits included balsa wood ribs, which were glued to a pre-cut balsa frame, then assembled, carefully glued together, and covered with a light tissue paper, decals, and paint, all to be hung from the bedroom ceiling when done. (Some planes had wind up rubber band motors, while advanced models had miniature motors.)

At the time, the government was promoting the advances and successes in flying as a way to build citizen morale in the country. Every new plane, its specifications and advantages, plus a silhouette for junior civilian defense spotters, was better promoted than many commercial products. For example, every boy knew that the P-38 Lightning could outfly a Japanese Zero fighter, or outduel a German Messerschmitt. Model buffs had memorized the specifications from Lockheed and knew the record "kills" made by the "forked tail devils." We seemed to think that by having our own model, even a plastic replica, we were part of the war effort. We also watched every plane that flew over the house, checked it against the civilian defense silhouette cards, and crazily hoped to be the first to spot a German bomber.

The patriotic fever associated with planes led us into, of all things, scrap collecting, a hobby that had us scouring the neighborhood for anything metal or rubber that could be reprocessed to help build planes and tanks for the troops overseas. My mother was quite unhappy when I appropriated a metal part of her sewing machine, one that she had to replace. My good intentions did not result in any mercy from her. We also collected newspapers, tied them up in bundles, and then sold all our treasures to the junk man who came around weekly with his old truck and scales—scales that seemed to always show less than we expected.

We used that money, or at least what was left over after buying a Baby Ruth candy bar, to buy savings stamps for the war effort. Each week we would try to have 10 cents for a stamp that we pasted in a book, which, once we had $18.75, could be turned in at the bank for a War Savings Bond that would eventually be redeemable for $25. Collecting Savings Bonds, as many movie stars and singers told us at the time, was a hobby that would help our troops win the war. Looking back, bonds did help unite the country.

Later, I joined the Boy Scouts, where collecting merit badges became a hobby, one that I enjoyed and which eventually allowed me to be an Eagle Scout. I enjoyed roughing it on the camping experiences, and I loved the jamborees. One exception was a scout jamboree where it rained so hard that our pup tent collapsed and we went home in the middle of the night. In another instance, the mosquitoes won a pitched battle, and in yet another we had a bear wandering around and retreated again. How did the Indians handle all this, we wondered? The scout program attempted to build character in young boys, so Mother was very supportive…until the scoutmaster asked me to take up the drums and be in their parade team. I took the intensity of her "absolutely not" comment as a definite no.

The allure of scouting has certainly changed. Today, at my age, roughing it means staying at a Holiday Inn; character building can only go so far.

2. MY FAVORITE HOBBIES

MY LIST	READER'S LIST —ADD YOUR FAVORITES
Stamp collection	
Coin collection	
Bag of marbles	
Decoder rings	
Butterfly displays	
Baseball trading cards	
Camping	
Model planes	
Model ships	
Collecting scrap metal	
War Bond savings stamps	
Lionel train sets	
Boy Scouts	
Airplane identification	
Singing in the choir	

3. TODAY AND TOMORROW

Today, a mother's need for children's hobby time is even greater than it was in our time, as she can no longer shoo everyone outside unless there is a guard or very large dog available. Instead of neighborhood playtime, kids are taken to organized activities such as sports or music, which means Mom is a full-time driver; it is almost as though she were the one being shooed outdoors. Consequently, Mom, despite all the timesaving appliances, now may have even less time to handle her duties than our mothers did. Her only recourse, just as her mother's before her, is to encourage in-house and backyard hobbies, hoping somehow these will soothe her savage children. And, if she is really lucky, the hobby may lead to a career.

Fortunately, in today's world, many "hobbies" come in electronic form, sometimes mirroring old hobbies we had. But in other cases, technology introduces entirely new hobbies with stunning, attention-holding visual effects. These hobbies are a boon to mothers for two reasons: first, the games do keep the kids occupied while in doors, relieving one worry, and second, the kids can be online with friends, so Mother does not need to be the unwilling playmate as she was in days of yore.

The computer is a hobby unto itself, one akin to exploring, but exploring the seemingly endless world of functions and features that are offered—whether they are useful or not. This "hobby" is almost a requirement for kids' education and future careers, as virtually every career has become dependent on this skill. Training thumbs to do text messaging, however, is not so important.

While electronic hobbies can be addictive, educational, and fun, the personal hobbies such as camping, stamp collecting, coin collecting, building models, singing, and many games such as marbles or checkers cannot be replaced by an electronic version, simply because the main pleasure of these activities derives from the physical engagement and the fun of face-to-face contact and personal negotiations. These person-to-person hobbies are more like dealing with real life, so having both types of hobbies may be the best solution.

Tomorrow, instead of building messy models kids may create a model holographic train set, which (and this can be done today) they then "print" on a 3D parts printer. (Just as a reality check, Jay Leno, whose hobby is antique cars, already has such a printer, which he uses to create spare auto parts.) In the future, a small home printer will build toys to your specifications. A bit scary.

On the other hand, we will see the end of stamp collecting, simply due to the fact that first class mail is disappearing and commercial mail uses uninteresting bar codes. BB guns, slingshots, and playing Indians have all become politically incorrect, so they will be replaced by ray guns and space cadets—things that have less baggage.

The Internet will also do things that Mother could not do, such as teach kids how to play an electronic guitar, to sing in perfect pitch and on tempo, and to become better chess players. Now if an online nanny will prepare the kids' meals and ensure each child eats the proper nutrients, mothers will really believe in progress!

The only thing we know for sure is that mothers will still need to encourage kids' (and husbands') hobbies if they are to maintain some peace and quiet in the home.

VACATIONS

Grandpa, what were your favorite vacations?

"There comes a time in every boy's life that he has a raging desire to go somewhere and dig for a buried treasure."

—Mark Twain

1. IT SEEMS LIKE ONLY YESTERDAY

While lying in my bed on a summer night with the window open, I could hear the train whistle in the far distance, and its haunting, long moan stirred my wanderlust for the romantic places I learned about from radio shows, movies, and books—places such as Gene Autry's Melody Ranch, Tarzan's dark jungles, or Terry and the Pirates' exploits in exotic China.

However, my young dreams and my parents' reality were far, far apart, separated by money and motivation. My grandparents had immigrated to America from the Canadian Maritimes, so their children's motivation was to find what their parents never had: stable work, a house of their own, and an education for their family. Vacations were not my parents' priority, and they were certainly not a priority of employers of that era, many of whom would have worked employees seven days a week if Sunday work had not been banned.

To make matters worse, Sunday church attendance was mandatory, partly due to Mother's rules and partly due to the fact that I sang in the boys' choir, which traveled to other churches several times a year. So between my parents' priorities and my own commitments, traveling and vacations were very limited. In fact, until I finished high school, I don't think my friends or I had ever been more than 100 miles from home. That is not to say that we did not have some delightful trips and short vacations, but rather that our travel was local—very local—and of very short duration.

When we were just tykes, our favorite place to go was Kimball's Ice Cream Ranch, a spot only 10 miles outside of town, where we enjoyed huge ice cream cones after taking a ride around a ring on a docile pony. I would wear my latest

Roy Rogers six-shooter guns and Gene Autry hat, pick a white steed, and give out the Lone Ranger's "Hi-Yo Silver, Away!"—probably convincing the poor pony that all kids were slightly crazy.

We also took day trips into New Hampshire, which seemed like a distant country to us, to visit the famous Benson's Wild Animal Farm (actually a training center for circus animals) and its many African elephants, gorillas, and lions. This was an environment where we felt very experienced, having been thoroughly educated by Tarzan movies and instructions from *Dr. Doolittle's Zoo*. We would take a picnic, watch the animals performing in the ring or just playing in their enclosures, and then, exhausted, we kids would sleep in the car's backseat all the way home.

I also spent many a Sunday building sand castles at the beach. There was one just a few miles away, and sometimes my parents took us on the ferry (which cost a nickel) to Nantasket Beach. Both locations had a boardwalk and Coney Island-like amusements. The bumper cars were my favorite, as they made me feel, at ten, that I was almost old enough to drive a car. The Ferris wheel and cyclone roller coaster were not as large as Coney Island's, but they were certainly high enough to frighten us nearly to death. The cyclone gave us bragging rights for about a week.

The amusement parks also came to us in the form of local carnivals, with their huge tents, flags, rides, and music. They sprung up overnight, adding a festival atmosphere to a nearby cow pasture. Neither Father's stern warnings about crooked games and pickpockets, nor the fact that I rarely won a prize did much to dampen my enthusiasm. I even went on nights when I had no money, just to revel in the excitement and, I suppose, think about the wandering life. I had read a book about a boy named Toby Tyler, who ran away to travel with the circus (and came home 10 weeks later), which provided an exciting question: would I dare follow his example, work with the animals, and eat "carney" food? Sadly, it turned out that my love of Mother's chocolate cake was greater than the call of adventure.

I suspect that my father had a degree of wanderlust as well, since he would drive us over to the nearby airport and spend several hours watching the planes take off and land. This was in the day of small single-engine planes, some with bi-wings, in which amateur pilots made bumpy landings on a grass airstrip and skywriters spewed smoke for a new advertising craze. I guess those trips stuck with me, as I eventually enlisted in the Air Force.

So trips were pretty local. Long automobile trips were a bit risky, as you may recall. Balloon tires on cars, combined with poor roads and mechanical brakes usually spelled trouble. Since gas stations were few and far between, taking kids on a long trip could hardly be classified as a vacation.

Father's big vacation interest, and one shared by Mother, was day-hiking in nearby mountains; a tough hobby when you have three small children. So when he was promoted and finally got vacations, we went to a rustic, lakeside cottage at Beaver Pond. I can still recall the towering pines, the low moan of the wind, and the beautiful call of the whip-poorwill, a sound rarely heard anymore. I recall my dad rowing on the lake in an old green rowboat with squeaky oarlocks—without a life preserver, of course. I also recall my brother, only three years old at the time, falling in the lake and my father running out on the dock, diving in, and rescuing him, an accident that shook up my mother more than my brother. These youthful outdoor experiences eventually encouraged me to join the Boy Scouts so that I could go camping in the woods and learn skills like swimming, a skill highly encouraged by my mother due to her memory of my brother's experience.

It was not until after high school, when I had my first full-time job, that I actually went on a vacation outside of New England. Two friends and I took the train to New York City and stayed in Times Square—which was affordable in those days—to see how the other half lived, and especially to visit Birdland to hear the legendary drummer, Gene Krupa and singer Sarah Vaughn. I am sure we looked like hicks, as we stared open-mouthed at the legendary buildings, bathed in the neon lights of Broadway, and ate at the famous Automat, which was all we could afford. We went home broke but seasoned travelers. That trip happened shortly before I enlisted for the Korean War, a period of time when I would have too many trips, but at Uncle Sam's expense.

The rest of my young wanderlust dreams, those that train whistles and reading had encouraged, amazingly did come true, but decades later than I had expected. For example, I now live in Gene Autry's Far West and have seen Terry and the Pirates' mysterious China, have been on safari in Tarzan's jungles of Africa, have hiked on Heidi's Swiss Alps, have strolled the streets of Oliver Twist's London, and have journeyed around Jack London's Alaska. This is living proof that one never knows where the road will take them.,(But dreaming sure helps.)

2. MY FAVORITE VACATIONS

MY LIST	READER'S LIST —ADD YOUR FAVORITES
Wild animal parks	
Town carnivals	
Horseback camp	
Scout jamboree	
Atlantic Ocean beaches	
Nantucket Island ferry	
Boston's Old Ironsides	
Paradox lakeside cottage	
Relatives' farms	
Mueller's Airport	
Times Square	
Grand Canyon	
Yellowstone	
Canoeing the Allagash in Maine	
Exploring the Canadian Maritimes	
Yosemite	

3. TODAY AND TOMORROW

Today, travel and vacations are a fundamental part of our culture. This is for a variety of reasons: the nomadic nature of our families, the highways that link every part of the nation, the relatively inexpensive cost of flying, the invention of rental cars, the proliferation of hotels and motels, and the far greater free time of parents. (Think about the fact that all those things are new in our lifetime!) Today, both parents probably work, but they tend to get several weeks of annual vacation time. They may have an RV or even a timeshare, and view vacations as a necessity.

One of the vacation options—getting the kids together with grandparents—has always been important, as these occasions help build family roots. However, in today's separated world, that vacation might require coast-to-coast travel. Long trips were pretty rare trip in our time; just recall that in the 1950s, a trip from Boston to New York took most of the day. A train from coast to coast was a good four days each way, a tough challenge with little children, just to see Grandpa. However, long distance travel for vacations is now the norm, partially driven by the fact that a child can't have a healthy upbringing if they have not been to Disneyland.

The entire idea of needing a vacation and "getting away from it all," once the province of the rich, seems to be today's answer to the complexity of daily life and sameness of urban living. Personally, I think vacations hurt more now than they did years ago; traffic is heavier, airline seats are smaller, lines are longer, food is not as good, and to add insult to injury, when you get home you must pay for the pleasure by dealing with the accumulated piles of e-mails and bills that are waiting for you! I can relate to author Elbert Hubbard's comment, "No man needs a vacation so much as the man who has just had one."

Tomorrow, with serious security concerns, the increasing cost of fuel, the pressure to protect your scarce job, and the world's growing population taxing every aspect of transportation, I expect vacations and travel problems will force our kids and grandkids to make more thoughtful decisions about vacations. However, somewhere in most people's breasts there is a wanderlust, and when they hear the far-off whistle blow, they will find a way to answer the call. Will better types of domestic travel emerge to replace cramped airplanes, slow ships, and slower trains? Will "beam me up" technology become real?

Or will the Jetsons' flying car finally become the answer to all our travel problems?

What we do know is that today's children will dream of new frontiers, just as we did, and those exotic frontiers will become more reachable with each generation. "Next stop Mars, anyone for Mars?"

FRIGHTENED

Grandpa, were you ever frightened you when you were growing up?

"Everyone gets afraid sometimes. It's what you do next that counts."

—Anonymous

1. IT SEEMS LIKE ONLY YESTERDAY

If anyone told me they were never frightened of anything, I would wonder whether they were exaggerating or whether they simply had never been away from their own home. Some folks say that they are brave and cannot be frightened, but that is simply confusing things, because being brave is facing up to something that *does* frighten you. Perhaps John Wayne said it best: "Bravery is being scared to death, but saddling up anyway."

When I was very young, I got scared after I read a story about monsters under our beds, or scary people hiding in the cellar. Despite Mother's assurances, I would always check things out before going to either place. Many young people slept soundly, but the unlucky ones had frightening night-mares, maybe about being chased by giant snakes—or in my case, due to a movie I saw, falling off the edge of the world into nowhere—only to wake with a frightened start. (Funny, years later my plane went down and I thought of those dreams; but fortunately, I never met the snakes.)

For my parents and grandparents, their greatest fears had more to do with the terrible illnesses that they had seen and whether a disease might harm their children. Most of us have forgotten the fear of yellow fever or cholera, agonizing diseases that left thousands dead and with no known cause. Then there was tuberculosis, which severely debilitated whoever got the bug, and scarlet and rheumatic fevers, with terrible rashes and fevers that lasted for weeks and sometimes left children scarred for life. In addition, there were the scary but rarely fatal problems of chicken pox, measles, mumps, and whooping cough to frighten them—and me as well, as I caught several of these diseases. Some of the original causes of these illnesses were poor water and hygiene, but once caught, they were highly contagious and might even subject the sick person to quarantine. I recall that for weeks I sadly looked out the window at neighborhood kids at play while I hid my face, which was covered with pox. It wasn't until later, in the 1930s when the miracle of antibiotic drugs was discovered and personal hygiene improved, that these diseases became more manageable. Prior to that, the only cure was time and your own immune system. (Disease had been one of the major reasons so many people migrated to the less crowded and more sanitary environment of the United States.) Even though medicine was getting more effective, especially after the '40s, our parents still recalled each disease's deadly history and feared for their children.

But the things that frightened me the most were scary movies! I suppose that is why we kept going back—we enjoyed the thrill of being frightened and yet surviving. The classic horror shows (mild by today's standards) such as *Dracula, The Hunchback of Notre Dame,* and *Dr. Jekyll and Mr. Hyde* would keep me wide-awake at night, jumping at every board that creaked or water pipe that clanked. Vincent Price in "House of Wax," or "Creature from the Black Lagoon," for example, had such frightening scenes that I can recall them even today.

Another thing that frightened most of us were bullies. A bully can be someone of any age who picks on others in order to feel more important. We had one such boy on our block who always picked on us, so we would either hide from him, humor him, or make sure we had a bigger boy with us when he came by. I was pretty small and pretty intimidated, but one day he took my new bat and would not return it when I asked. Instead he bent down to take my baseball, as well. I was so mad that I forgot I was frightened and while he was bent over, I gave him a hard kick in the seat of his pants. I then turned and ran as fast as I could, figuring he would get me later, but a quick victory and strategic retreat was the smart move now. What I did not see was the kicked bully losing his balance and falling over the low wall into the rose bush, getting all scratched up and going home crying—without my bat or ball! He never bothered me again and I learned the value of standing tall, and also, surprisingly, that I had more courage than I thought.

We all encounter bullies throughout our lives and must find ways to deal with them, or else constantly live in fear. A bully can be a playmate, teacher, boss, coworker, bureaucrat, neighbor, or even a relative. I learned that you couldn't kick them all in the rear end, much as I might have liked the idea. After a while, I learned that there are many types of bullies and each one needs to be handled in a different way; this becomes a big part of what is called "street smarts," a subject too long for this book.

Mother was not always helpful regarding bravery, making a big deal over every scratch I got, which felt good but was the wrong approach for a boy. By contrast, I recall my dad insisting I get up when I fall; he'd make me try again and never give up. He took me to a movie—one whose name I cannot recall—where a cowboy kept getting thrown off his horse, only to get back on until the horse, obviously the stronger of the two, gave up and became gentle. Decades later, after a frightening plane accident, I actually used my father's "get back in the saddle" lesson to curb my fear of flying, by forcing myself, white knuckles and all, to go up in a glider—a lesson in overcoming fear that worked just the way he said it would.

Way back, I recall being terrified when I went to school for the first time. Mother left me there with strangers (teachers) and went home. I felt she had betrayed me and that I was doomed (at least until the teacher gave me a brownie). Later, in third grade I had to recite a poem in front of all the students and parents, and again I felt the fear of being alone, the fear of failure. But with Mother in the audience, I somehow overcame the fear and survived.

After high school, I was not quite that frightened, but still very unsure when I left home and went first into the military and then later to college. In both cases, the protective shield of my parents' love had been taken away and I was on my own, a new venture into the unknown. Was I up to it? Did I know enough? Would people like me? What if I flunked out? Would I be frightened if I went into combat? My answer to all of them was yes, but somehow I made my way? A few years later, I drove in stock car races, a sport that has been described as boredom interspersed with moments of sheer terror, yet every driver "saddles up" again, overcoming their fear, because they have grown more confident in their abilities.

There are many frightening things where we have no control over the outcome. In some of these cases, such as the years we feared an atomic war with Russia, it requires both bravery and optimism. The combination of these two traits offers a shield against many problems. However, they do not help with monsters under the bed.

I was frightened many times, as were many of my friends, but in most cases we simply kept going forward, with a lot of help from others. I think most of us found that we were a lot tougher than Mother thought we were.

2. MY FRIGHTENING THINGS

MY LIST	READER'S LIST —ADD YOUR FAVORITES
Monsters under the Bed	
First day of school	
Getting lost	
Daddy's belt	
The Wolfman	
Horror shows	
Bullies	
Final exams	
Accidents	
Heights	
Serious illness	
High speed	
Mean bosses	

3. TODAY AND TOMORROW

Today, the diseases our parents (and we) used to fear are far less frequent, thanks to medicine and scientific breakthroughs. Many things that used to cause accidents have been legislated away. The anti-bullying educational programs of the past decade have reduced this problem, but certainly not eliminated it. However, it seems a parent's life is always one of fear. A few decades ago we feared for our children's safety in a world threatened by nuclear war with Russia, and went through the bomb shelter period. Today the fear of terrorism, perverts, drugs, obesity, behavioral issues, or societal disease are far greater dangers than in our era, and those fears continue to turn a mother's hair prematurely grey.

In some ways, the challenge parents face has not changed. For example, how do you advise a child when to be brave and when to make a strategic retreat? Will the child be brave on the roller coaster and yet be afraid to face a bully? Will a child be so afraid of criticism that they will avoid risk? Will they be too brave, or simply not respect danger? The development of "street smarts," and the wisdom and common sense surrounding bravery and fear, wisdom that must be imparted or encouraged by grownups and friends, may determine a child's future. In the meantime, kids keep on doing what kids do, just like we did.

Tomorrow, there will still be many things worth fearing. After all, if progress continues at this pace, our grandchildren will be asked to take spaceships to galaxies we have yet to discover; they may find mining jobs at the bottom of the sea or may have to fight giant robots in defense of mankind. Whatever happens, their courage in frightening situations, just like our courage, will shape the future.

But just remember what Christopher Robin wisely said to Pooh, and which I urge you to pass on: "Promise me you'll always remember: You're braver than you believe, and stronger than you seem, and smarter than you think."

SECTION TWO

SCHOOL DAYS

"Too many people grow up. That's the trouble with the world;
they don't remember what it was like to be twelve years old."

—Walt Disney

Growing pains are part of that wonderful, awful period of time when life throws many different experiences at us in rapid succession, each experience adding a new dimension to what was once a simple, pleasant life. From middle school through high school, we simultaneously attempt to get out from the shadow of our parents, convince everyone that we are special, and prove we are uniquely capable of dealing with life. It is a bit like attempting to fly before growing wings.

This is a period when sports becomes an obsession, when members of the opposite sex suddenly become important, when clothes and looks become crucial to acceptance, when a bedroom becomes a personal territory, and when we come to the startling and self-serving conclusion that we know more than our old-fashioned parents.

It is also a time of pain, when a third strike means the end of the world, a cute girl's refusal to go to a dance with you makes living any longer a waste of time, when a boy's ability to shave or get a license proves his manhood, when your acceptance by the "in-crowd" defines who you really are, and when you would not be caught dead with your hair uncombed (or combed, depending on the current fad).

While all that is going on, you must figure out what you are going to be when you grow up, whether you are willing to pay the price to attain that goal, determine how to convince your folks to pay for it and still claim, straight-faced, to be an independent person.

Go back with me now to those rich adolescent years where school, sports, music, and friends were totally unique, totally chaotic, and totally memorable.

SCHOOL SUBJECTS

Grandpa, what were your favorite and least favorite school subjects when you were a boy?

"My school was so tough, the school newspaper had an obituary section."

—**Bill Cosby**

1. IT SEEMS LIKE ONLY YESTERDAY

I suppose the glib answer, "my favorite subjects were recess and gym," would not really be true, because I liked study hall, too. My favorite subjects were usually determined by my family's ideas, my own reading of books, my own nature, and how well a teacher motivated the class. There were some teachers who could pass on their passion about a subject and inspire a student so much that that they really paid attention. For example, our fifth grade teacher, Mrs. Hawks, was passionate about birds, trees, and geography, and she utilized these subjects as a basis for art classes, storytelling, and reading assignments. She inspired me to join the Boy Scouts and her love of nature stayed with me throughout the years. The same was true in high school mathematics, where two of my teachers turned the usually tough subjects of geometry and algebra into practical ways to solve real problems. The fun of finding a solution almost overcame the burden of the homework and in the long run provided a somewhat logical way of thinking.

But then there were teachers who were tired of trying; even young and motivated teachers got exhausted. For example, in junior high school, one new teacher we had was young and very attractive, and a few of the unruly kids in the class made embarrassing comments about her figure. One day, her fiancé visited our classroom. He could only make it through the classroom doorway by turning his broad shoulders sideways. Topping 300 pounds, Gino was then playing guard for professional football's Philadelphia Eagles. He just said hello, looked around the room, and left, but the teacher never had a problem controlling the boys after that lesson. Gino's presence was inspirational.

School sports created some special, life-deciding problems for me—not because I had the potential to play for the Eagles, but because if Latin classes created a schedule conflict or demanded too much homework, thereby interfering with a chosen sport, the choice seemed simple. The fact that Latin might help me learn languages for the rest of my life was not as obvious a benefit as the immediate popularity I could gain by playing a sport. Much to my chagrin, wiser heads usually prevailed.

Wiser heads were also needed for the choice of major curriculum. Our school had four broad paths to choose from: one option was a group of college preparatory courses, which were essential for acceptance at a major college and were, obviously, the toughest and had the most homework; the second was a general course, aimed at the undecided students; the commercial course was primarily for secretarial and homemaking skills; and finally we could choose the trade curriculum.

The trade curriculum included job training in auto mechanics, sheet metal work, and carpentry, to name a few. (Computers did not exist at that time, otherwise programming might have made the list.) For many boys, working on or "souping-up" your car was one of the most important things in their young lives, which gave the trade courses a special appeal. Of course, minimal homework requirements provided another strong inducement.

In addition, these trade courses were appealing to many parents, whose fondest hope was to have their getting-more-expensive-every-year children to be self-supporting as fast as possible. For some parents, keeping up with growing appetites and supporting the style-conscious teens was a huge burden.

But some kids had parents who were trying to escape the trades, which meant taking the college courses whether we liked it or not. In my case, Mother spoke and I listened; the alternative—disobeying—would be like volunteering for all the chores she could dream up...forever.

There were some courses I really disliked, but I could only sway Mother on a few of them. One that I suffered through was the Palmer Method of cursive handwriting; good handwriting was a necessary tool in our lives and one that reflected on a person's refinement. However, Palmer had taken rote learning to great heights, forcing us to scribe letters such as "A" several hundred times, using a wooden pen, nib, and inkwell, invariably causing ink-stained fingers. (No one seemed to connect the fact that a common school punishment was to write 100 times "I will not talk in class," or some such confession, and yet Palmer seemed to think that repetitive writing of the letter "A" was a joyful learning experience. Very strange, but what did I know?) Handwriting ranks as my most disliked course of all time.

My other least favorite subject was chemistry, through no fault of any teacher. We lived near a Monsanto plant, and the odors from the piles of yellow sulfur and other chemicals wafted across the city in the summer, killing any desire to be in that business. If that was not bad enough, the chemistry classroom in our old school held decades-old odors that made a student's eyes water. Another pet peeve was the civics course (taught by our football coach and attended by jocks) which, as I found years later, is a fascinating and important subject if you have a passionate teacher, but is dullsville otherwise.

Another course that I avoided was biology, but that was just my own doing. When we dissected a worm I was okay, but they lost me when we got to the frogs. Years later I lived on a farm for a while and very quickly learned not to be so squeamish. Once you help a cow give birth, dissecting frogs is a piece of cake.

I also disliked public speaking—a required course—because I was a bit shy. However, I was very fortunate and had a teacher who must have been an Army sergeant at one time. He brooked no excuses or half-hearted efforts and would stay after school with me until I polished my "style" to his satisfaction. In later years, that skill served me extremely well.

My favorite subject of all was literature, not so much due to the teacher's style but because he chose wonderful books and provided insightful comments about the plots and structure. For avid readers, this was not homework but something we wanted to do anyway, making the course a real favorite. (I do recall the teacher being quite annoyed when he found two female students reading *Movie Weekly* rather than Shakespeare, but it was a tough city, after all.) For me, writing a book report was a pleasure—as long as they did not grade my penmanship.

Looking back, I realize how many times my parents stepped in, forbid me to take the easy way out, and stood firm on the importance of good education. Such old-fashioned folks!

2. SCHOOL SUBJECTS

SUBJECTS I ENJOYED	READER'S LIST
Geography	
History	
Algebra	
English	
Civics	
Literature	
Biology	
Art	

Shop
Gym
Geometry

3. TODAY AND TOMORROW

Today, thanks to electronics, children can learn more about more things than we ever did, but in some ways they might learn less. I am sure that watching and hearing a video, presumably created by an expert, can impart more knowledge in a shorter period of time and achieve greater retention than a local teacher and a blackboard. In addition, a student can go on the Internet and research any subject in a matter of minutes, usually making homework more manageable and containing more depth of materials.

Learning history, for example, would seem to be far more pleasant and have greater staying power, if you were watching a documentary that made Gettysburg a living thing, rather than simply memorizing the dates. Many years after my rather boring high school history class, I took a mandatory college course in humanities, with a large part of the material focusing on ancient Greece. The professor was Greek and taught with such passion that the characters in his lectures came alive; you could almost feel the noise of the ancient battles and the fear of a tragic voyage when he spoke. Due to him, Greek mythology remains a favorite subject of mine even today. If he had been able to use videos instead of photos, it would have been even better. Then students everywhere could have felt his passion.

Apparently penmanship is no longer taught in school, the computer keyboards replacing the Parker pens, which had already replaced inkwells. And if you have read any handwritten thank you notes from young people then you know what I meant by "learning less."

Learning less is a real worry, especially in the area of problem solving. I recall learning trigonometry theorems and formulas, especially how they worked, and then solving problems, first with a slide rule and later with a hand calculator. Today, you simply enter a problem statement and the computer provides the answer, without any prerequisite knowledge of the inner workings. The same might be true of learning how to repair a car or a myriad of other problems. Maybe it is just my view, but children need to learn the how, when, and where as well as what to do. Without any background knowledge, anyone can push a button, but they will never appreciate which genie they may have unleashed.

Tomorrow, I suspect that most classes will be taught online, by the person who is judged to be the greatest teacher in that subject, no matter where they are in the world. Classrooms will be focused on discussions, led by a local teacher, and some electronic scanning device will do testing. Homework will be submitted online and graded by a robotic reader, thereby eliminating parents' complaints that poor Johnny was unfairly graded and making teachers' lives far more pleasant.

My greatest hope is that our grandchildren will enjoy a new education paradigm, one with courses in logic, common sense, ethics, and thinking that will help them make a better world. For, as our parents knew, education must have two equally important components to be successful. One is how to make a living, and the other is how to live.

SPORTS

Grandpa, did you play sports in school?

"I wanted to be a sportswriter because although I loved sports, I could not hit the curve ball, the jump shot, or the opposing ball carrier."

—Dick Schaap, sportswriter, broadcaster, and author

1. IT SEEMS LIKE ONLY YESTERDAY

When I was young, there were no Little League or Pop Warner teams in my town, so we had no organized training, no videos, and not even batting cages to help us improve our skills. Our pick-up games might have used an old baseball wrapped in tape, a burlap bag for second base, and hand-me-down gloves and bats, but it was pure fun. However, the city did organize summer "sandlot leagues" in baseball and fall basketball, primarily as a way to keep kids busy and out of trouble. Our neighborhood park played other neighborhood parks with the help of a part-time coach, whose main job was to umpire and stop arguments. Working fathers rarely attended a game, which might have been a blessing.

The city parks program had a very motivational arrangement with the Boston Braves called the "Knothole Gang," which gave a few kids free game passes to the bleachers on slow weekdays. This was a real thrill, a chance to see the greatest left-handed pitcher in baseball, Warren Spahn. It made most of us fans forever; we knew all his statistics (363 career wins!) and even how he held a baseball. I still recall some of the old Braves line up, with shortstop Sibby Sisti, clutch-hitting Tommy Holmes, catcher Phil Masi, and the improbably named outfielder Clyde Kluttz. We all tried to emulate our heroes' styles, and as a result baseball became a lifelong obsession—a love affair that even survived the heartbreak of the Braves leaving Boston in 1953. That divorce forced us to reluctantly switch our allegiance to Ted Williams and the long suffering Boston Red Sox.

The sports of that day had logical seasons, unlike today's endless, overlapping, distracting seasons. Baseball began on April 1 and the World Series ended in September, just as the football teams got underway. Then as winter set in, football ended and basketball and hockey began and filled in the dreary months (although I am sure that these sports realized they were simply a distraction from the real Boston passion, baseball).

Professional football, at the time, was in its infancy, and we had a lackluster team called the Boston Yanks, which did not inspire any fan base. Instead, college football held everyone's attention—especially teams like Notre Dame, with its legendary "Four Horsemen" under Knute Rockne, or Army's Doc Blanchard and Glenn Davis (Mr. Outside and Mr. Inside) and their coach Earl "Red" Blaik. Then there was "Slingin' Sammy" Baugh of Texas Christian University, one of the all-time greats, who led the college All Stars to a win over the Green Bay Packers; he then signed with the Washington Redskins for the amazing bonus of $4,000! Great college ball was the name of the game until Thanksgiving rolled around.

Professional basketball was the opposite situation, at least in our area. The heartland and southern colleges had intense followings of college basketball and still do today. But in the Northeast, the Celtics, behind Bob Cousy, Phil Sharman, Bill Russell, and KC Jones, dominated fan attention with eleven championships in a thirteen-year period. I would spend hours at the local gym trying to duplicate Bob Cousy's set shot (only worth two points back then) or perfect that behind-the-back dribble he used so well. However, after all that practice, I got an "A" for effort but only a "C" for execution.

Unfortunately for me, I was never a star athlete in any sport, a shortcoming that was heartbreaking at the time, creating a feeling that I was doomed to a life of failure and, even worse, that I would never date the prettiest girls in school, as they all seemed attracted to the campus stars. I recall that I enjoyed football, but like many high schools around the country, we had very large children from second-generation families or farm families. In my junior year in high school, our football team's front line outweighed the Green Bay Packer's front line. I weighed all of 150 pounds at the time, and our right guard equaled two of me at 300 pounds, making the coach invite me to be a water boy. So I played sandlot football on a team sponsored by our local barber, a man named "Bitzi," whose brother played in the pros. When we had an undefeated season, thanks to two speedy running backs named Joe and Jerry, he gave us team jackets with his name on the back. My mother was a bit unhappy, as Bitzi also ran the local numbers racket. And so it goes in sports.

Then suddenly, in the tenth grade, to my delight I began to grow and grow, tacking on six inches of height in two years; in my senior year, I became a prospect for the basketball team. (Of course that growth was a disaster for my parents, who seemed to have to buy me new clothes on a weekly basis, and displeased my brother who, given my hogging of the family clothes budget, had to inherit the hand-me-downs.) Unfortunately, the growth spurt came too late in high school to help me make the varsity teams. However, I was lucky to play town ball on a very good team, and later I played on an Air Force base team. In one thrilling event, our US Air Force base team played a preliminary game, just before the main game, with the Harlem Globetrotters—an experience that quickly showed me that I had a lot to learn. We also played a semiprofessional women's team called the Dallas Cowgirls. The forward I was covering was six inches taller than I was, and at tip-off, when she leaned over and kissed me on top of the head, I knew I was going to have a tough night. We barely won the game, as I recall, but that may be a convenient memory.

The big sports in our high school were almost exclusively baseball, basketball, and football, as there were no facilities for tennis, golf, or hockey, and no indoor swimming pool for aquatics teams. As you would expect, football and basketball had cheerleaders and drew large crowds of students and parents, and also, therefore, financial aid. Competition with rival cities, especially the Thanksgiving cross-town football rivalry, would raise tempers and passions to all-time highs, inspiring fights in the stands, the tearing down of goal posts, and other pranks that were considered obligatory actions by the students. This was despite stern game-prep warnings from both of the school principals. However, passionate fans seemed to encourage great athletic efforts and great games, which resulted in several of my classmates winning football scholarships to very good universities.

The high school baseball team, on the other hand, had to compete for the attention of student ballplayers with the well-organized American Legion Baseball league; the Legion supported thousands of local youth teams in most large cities and towns across the country. The American Legion was supported by the major leagues and had earned a reputation for getting young, promising players professional contracts (Bob Feller, for one) and college scholarships; those dreams attracted the best of our high school players. The dreams also attracted a lot of parents to the Legion games, far more than went to high school games. Two of my friends starred in "Legion Ball" and made it to farm teams; one received a scholarship; but no one made the big leagues. I was sure that I "could have been a contender", if they had just outlawed curve balls and lefties.

By my first two years in college, I had gained enough height and weight to play sports, but my course workload, plus working downtown twenty hours a week, did not leave much free time. (Those were the days when we could work our way through college, without a huge loan.) Fortunately, by my junior year, I won a few scholarships to pay the college bills, and that freed up some fun time.

In my sophomore year, a friend introduced me to college golf, and by my senior year I just barely made the varsity team—a team that had part of its spring training at beautiful Pinehurst, North Carolina. After that experience, I was hooked on golf forever. It was a sport that I would pursue for the next 50 years and which I will never master, a sport where height and weight mean very little, and a sport where, especially when you are older, a glorious day and a beautiful course seems more important than any errors you might make. This is very good thing, as I seem to make a few more errors every passing year.

Golf was a good turning point in my sports life, because it is a sport I can still play fairly well. At my age, with my old knees, senior basketball and tennis are spectator sports. I might add that golf may be a more physically tolerant sport, but it grows psychologically tougher as you age. Now I mentally suffer from bogies every week and have found no cure.

2. SPORTS HIGHLIGHTS

MY LIST OF FAVORITE MEMORIES	READER'S LIST
Basketball recreation league	
Sandlot baseball	
American Legion baseball	
High school basketball	
Sports equipment/ uniforms	
School rivalries	
Pep rallies	
Cheerleaders	

Sports jackets/lettering	
USAF base team	
Doubles tennis	
Great golf courses	
The Boston Celtics	
Bob Cousy	
Warren Spahn	
Ted Williams	

3. TODAY AND TOMORROW

Today, the well-organized Little Leagues, the amount of coaching available, the mechanical aids (such as video replay lessons), and the almost scientific dissection of the mechanics of a sport all provide a far different experience than our "hit and miss" approach to sports. For kids who are small or young, there are plenty of options to participate and grow in all kinds of activities. In fact, I find that watching a Little League game or Pee Wee football can be even more entertaining than watching the pros. Talk about hustle!

However, children's sports have made parental life more difficult, especially for working parents who must act as a chauffeur to a multitude of events, a cheerleader even when they're tired, and a psychologist for bruised egos. Unlike our cross-town sandlot games, the kids must travel far and wide to compete in soccer, track, tennis, or swimming. This means that parents must become skilled chauffeurs or at least car pool coordinators throughout the school year. Sometimes parents do this in hopes of a great scholarship or, wonder of wonders, a professional contract for their child, which would put everyone in the family on the elusive "Easy Street." Or, failing stardom, it is referred to as helping a kid's social development. (Did I mention the cost of all the uniforms, shoes and gear?)

While life may be more difficult for parents, it may be true for the children as well. The young potential superstar receives a lot more direction from a lot of coaches. Being told what to do is not what kids usually enjoy. Also, the proximity of parental cheerleaders may introduce too high a level of pressure too early in their sports careers. For example, who wants to discuss missing a third strike or missed basket over dinner? On balance, however, kids today are learning more and learning earlier than we did, and hopefully that will help them enjoy the many rewards of sports for years to come.

Tomorrow may bring some big changes. Maybe my old high school will have a 400-pound lineman! And, if kids keep growing taller, we will have to raise the height of baskets in basketball, or maybe move the Little League mound back a ways and devise armor plating (like knights of old) for football players. Or alternatively, we may have robots playing as NFL linemen who, like the bionic man, have had all their vulnerable parts replaced with ceramics. Great idea! Then they could play football every Sunday, all year long. My wife can hardly wait!

MUSIC

Grandpa, what was your favorite music?

"As long as there is a song in your heart, you will always have hopes and dreams."

—Anonymous

1. IT SEEMS LIKE ONLY YESTERDAY

Everyone's musical taste is amazingly different and yet no one is right or wrong, as most musical tastes are developed according to the era and environment in which you lived. For example, if you grew up in some areas of the South and Midwest, the gospel, blues, and country music on *Grand Ole Opry* or *National Barn Dance* might have influenced you. That was when Red Foley, Hank Williams, and Lester Flatt got everyone's toes tapping. Or, if you lived in the big city environment of New York, you might have been influenced by the jazz and beats of Harlem, with Cab Calloway, Duke Ellington, Fats Domino, and the mellow tones of the Ames Brothers. I still recall seeing Ella Fitzgerald singing "How High the Moon" and Sara Vaughn doing "Misty."

In Manhattan, the great Rogers and Hammerstein gave us such classic Broadway musicals as *Oklahoma, The King and I,* and *The Sound of Music,* creating musical memories that will influence us forever. Sometimes, parental tastes—maybe influenced by Enrico Caruso—encouraged our love of opera, or molded our like or dislike of Big Band sounds from Benny Goodman or Jimmy Dorsey. No matter which style of music you preferred, we were blessed with memorable music and memorable performers throughout our youth.

My early musical education came from listening to radio shows of popular music from the late 1930s, but that was only when my family's first priorities, namely adventure stories and the news, were off the air. However, I was also influenced by church music, fulfilling one of Mother's dreams by becoming a boy soprano soloist. The music in church could be pretty spectacular (and frightening for the singer), especially singing the high notes of "Ave Maria" or "O Holy Night." I could reach those notes, so Mother had great hopes for me. Then one day my voice broke, as young men's do, and I was sud-

98

denly an alto! Mother never quite forgave me for messing up her career plan for me.

Another big influence on our young musical tastes must have been the movies, which for boys included Westerns. For example, when Hollywood Westerns introduced singing cowboys, we were appalled at this offense, this "sissification" of our hard-nosed, iron-fisted heroes. But as time went by, Gene Autry's Western classic "Back In the Saddle Again" was grudgingly accepted. Even today, "Tumbling Tumbleweeds" and "Cool Water" by the Sons of the Pioneers (who were supposedly simple ranch hands with miraculous harmony) and "Don't Fence Me In" by Roy Rogers are still among my all-time favorite tunes. Other movie music that I recall includes Gene Kelly's "Singing in the Rain" and Bing's "White Christmas." Imagine! Singers sang songs whose lyrics we could understand!

As young boys, we had little use for mushy songs—or for girls, for that matter, who seemed to be put here on Earth to annoy us; men, as everyone knew, should be more interested in horses. We were more attuned to Fess Parker singing "Davey Crockett, King of the Wild Frontier," Bing Crosby's rendition of "I'm an Old Cow Hand," "Get Along Little Dogies" by Roy Rogers, fun songs like "Zip-a-Dee-Do-Dah," or even Judy Garland singing "We're Off to See the Wizard." No mushy stuff for "us guys."

As we got a bit older and WWII erupted, our heroes changed and we turned to more patriotic music, such as the Andrew Sisters singing "Any Bonds Today?", Bing's rendition of "Coming in on a Wing and a Prayer," Kate Smith's "God Bless America," and Kay Kyser playing "Praise the Lord and Pass the Ammunition," not to mention all of John Phillip Sousa's marches. (You might recall Pat Boone's hit "Dear John," about the lost love of a soldier, as a mushy hit.) Truth be told, music and movies played a big role in uniting the country; they also played a big role in keeping young folks patriotic enough to contribute to the war effort through war bonds, civil defense, and victory gardens. In that era, a Fourth of July parade actually brought tears to the eyes of the onlookers. A great feeling.

Recorded music for home use had been around since the turn of the century. You may recall the old name *Gramophone*, which was the German firm that made the big, early record players. They were bought out by Victor, which later merged into the famous company with the dog logo, RCA. In the 1940s, just in time for the returning GIs, RCA brought out new twelve-inch long-play (LP) vinyl records, which had an amazing twenty minutes on each side! These replaced the old carbon records that scratched and shattered pretty easily. More progress brought us the smaller ten-inch "45s," and then the light, seven-inch 33rpm plastic disks that we carried along with our portable phonograph players. Today, some of our kids have never seen a portable phonograph, needles, or records. (However, many folks with a "good ear" still like the old records' warmer sound; aficionados bought 3 million vinyl records last year.)

As the war ground to a close (and recorded music was finally used for broadcasts), popular music was aimed at the returning servicemen and their hopeful loved ones. Suddenly, recorded music was in soda shops on jukeboxes, music-only radio stations, and in the "musical" movies. Best of all was the music played at "starlight ballrooms". These were outdoor dance floors where live bands, such as Artie Shaw, or local disk jockeys drew huge crowds of returning GIs every weekend. My own favorite ballroom locations, in later years, were in New Hampshire, Boston and Denver. What could be better than great music, a moon and stars and a pretty girl in your arms? Well, one thing maybe. I recall that I met a beautiful girl at one dance and was quite smitten. However, after I stepped on her toes twice, our romance quickly ended. Obviously she did not see my finer points.

Of course, by that time, I had "matured" to my early teens, and girls had gone from a nuisance to a grudging necessity, so my musical tastes had changed as well. Vaughn Monroe's "Ghost Riders In The Sky" became less important than, say, Ezio Pinza's soaring voice on "Some Enchanted Evening," or the Ames Brothers crooning "Sentimental Me."

The *Your Hit Parade* on radio—and eventually TV— became a big deal, with Frank Sinatra at first, and then Snooky Lanson and Dorothy Collins. If you missed the latest tunes on Hit Parade, you were simply not "Hep." Local dances featured the smooth, slow songs of Bing Crosby, Tony Bennett, Teresa Brewer, Perry Como, Doris Day, Billy Eckstine, and Pat Boone, songs that were better for the clumsy feet of most of the guys. That style of music also meant holding the girl close to you, with an emphasis on shared emotions. The art of dancing separately was, in our convenient opinion, reserved for "showboaters."

Speaking of showboaters, none of my friends could understand the female attraction to Frank Sinatra. We measured guys by how strong they were, how well the played ball and other macho measures. Why the girls screamed and swooned over a guy to thin to be water-boy and not very good looking, was a mystery we never solved.

A few years later we entered an era when up-tempo acts like Chubby Checker and Bobby Darin, and folk singers such as the Kingston Trio and Peter, Paul, and Mary were monopolizing the airwaves. (Years later, Elvis, with his mixture of gospel and rockabilly, would change music forever.) Along about that time, I had begun to take more interest in dances—as long as they did not interfere with sports events (the big league dreams were still the dominant factor in my young life). However, the new dances were a problem for my challenged feet. For example, I could fake it for waltzes and foxtrots, but when we got to the jitterbug, the twist, or even the rumba, they were not "playing my song"! Somehow, music did not travel from my head to my feet, a physical disability I have never been able to cure.

The movies I watched had also changed, as most dates would rather see a musical like *Oklahoma!* than the *Night of the Living Dead*. The only mutually enjoyable musicals were *Yankee Doodle Dandy*, with Jimmy Cagney, and the easy-to-relate-to *West Side Story* with Natalie Wood. Both movies helped save our tough-guy images, so it did not appear that we were surrendering to mushy music.

There is also a special place in my memories for the fun songs of the era, some with words that could not be understood, such as "Mairzy Doats." (In this case, of course, the mushing-together of the words—"mares eat oats"—was done on purpose, unlike some current music where the singers unintentionally achieve the same result.) In addition to fun songs that utilized play-on-words effects, the very talented but comedic band of Spike Jones took great joy in adding their unique sound effects to a musical score. The Spike Jones rendition of the romantic song "Cocktails for Two" was an example of a murderous masterpiece that emphasized chaos and was only mildly recognizable from the original score. The supposedly romantic song included cowbells, sirens, horns, gurgling, and more. The original composer was furious. Along with Doodles Weaver, Spike sometimes added words to popular tunes. One featured Doodles as an announcer at a race track with Spike's "William Tell Overture" in the background; Girdle was leading in the stretch, Banana was in the bunch, and the winner was Beetle Baum. This crazy music was aiming to entertain, not to establish a true musical genre. (Mike Wallace was Spike's MC!)

Music of the '50s is still among my favorites; I suppose that music of your high school years stays with you, whatever it is. But we had some undeniably memorable music—Frankie

Lane (recall Mule Train?), Nat King Cole, The Mills Brothers, The Ink Spots, The Ames Brothers, The Supremes, The Kingston Trio, Pearl Bailey, Patsy Kline, the beginning of the doo-wop sound, and so much more. Beautiful sounds, great lyrics and smooth dance music—usually.

Once again, I am sure our grandkids can't imagine how we survived high school in such a primitive musical era, an era called B.B. (Before the Beatles), and without rock 'n' roll. In 1962, the Decca recording company (people from my generation) said, upon rejecting The Beatles, "We don't like their sound, and guitar music is on the way out." No wonder that both Elvis Presley and The Beatles purposefully waited until my friends and I graduated before they made an appearance. Maybe they realized we lacked the mobile hips and feet that their music required, and they simply waited for a more flexible audience.

During the '60s, a new era of entertainers captured the upcoming generation. Their stars ranged from the Jefferson Airplane to Lovin' Spoonful to Bob Dylan, and the Beach Boys. Somehow, I lost interest. I think Bill Haley and "Blue Suede Shoes" seems to have been the point I got lost. But I recall one special man who just went with the flow no matter the music genre. That was Dick Clark; teenage girls (of any age) watched his show, American Bandstand, for decades. Maybe that is what kept him looking so young.

Through all the years, music in many forms played an important role in everyone's life, some more than others. For those who studied music, they gained special skills in memorization, perseverance, preciseness, and even teamwork (assuming they played in a band or an orchestra). In some cases, good dancing won a fair lady, and in others it created a wonderful hobby. But for all of us, music, through its stories and rhythms, did more to shape our generation than people realize. After all, if music could have an impact on someone like me, with two left feet and a breaking alto voice, who was safe?

2. MY FAVORITE MUSIC

MY LIST	READER'S LIST ARTISTS
Roy Rogers	
Gene Autry	
Bing Crosby	
Ted Lewis	
Danny Kaye	
Spike Jones	
Patti Page	
Mills Brothers	
Ink Spots	
Vaughn Monroe	
Andrews Sisters	
Glenn Miller	
Perry Como	
Kay Starr	
Songs	
Me and My Shadow	
Racing With The Moon	
Tumbling Tumbleweeds	
Don't Fence Me In	
Mule Train	
Swinging on a Star	
Chattanooga Shoe Shine Boy	
Lazy River	
Sentimental Journey	
Ole Buttermilk Sky	

I'll Walk Alone
I'm Looking Over a Four Leaf Clover
Oklahoma
Alexander's Ragtime Band
Coming in on a Wing and a Prayer
Some Enchanted Evening
The Wheel of Fortune
Fun Songs
Der Fuehrer's Face (Spike Jones)
Zip-a-Dee-Doo-Dah (Johnny Mercer)
Mairzy Doats (Merry Macs)
I'm My Own Grandpa (Phil Harris)
The Thing (Phil Harris)
Pistol Packin' Momma (Al Dexter)
Shoo Fly Pie (Dinah Shore)
If I Knew You Were Comin' I'd've Baked a Cake (Eileen Barton)
Military
American Patrol
Bell Bottom Trousers
Off We Go

Here are some great examples of the music we loved:
http://backwhen.com/MemorableMusic.html

3. TODAY AND TOMORROW

Today, fortunately for us, recording technology allows us to listen to any artist and any song from any period or genre that we find pleasing. Instead of large radios or big turntables and unwieldy records, we can store an extraordinary number of tunes on our iPod and similar devices. The journey that got us here was built on creative minds that led us on a trip through console radios, vinyl records, cassette tapes, CDs, DVDs, and memory chips, all in an effort to bring us music, music, music. Even the venerable jukebox, which began as a mechanical device that flipped platters onto turntables, is now an online device with thousands of digital musical selections.

I currently have about four hundred songs on my iPod, and many of my friends have even more. As a way to look at the technical progress we have made in this area, think of carrying around a case of four hundred single song (45rpm) records in one arm and the player in the other. Drop them and you had a disaster. Think about the chore of finding a specific singer or song from that pile, versus today when you simply scroll to the song or artist and hit "play." Think also of scratched records and worn record needles, or the frustration of a tangled cassette tape. We replaced all of that with a pretty rugged unit the size of a calling card. Incredible!

I have learned that technical progress always has a flip side. In this case, musical instrument technology encourages performers to show how loud an instrument can be played— the sound drowning out any hope of understanding the lyrics. (Which in some cases may be a blessing.) And maybe it is just my bad hearing, but even on recordings where the instruments are not as loud, singers apparently don't feel clear diction is a worthy goal; instead, it seems that many singers must be paid for how loud they scream...I mean sing. I realize that we had songs where the words made no sense, such as "When the moon hits your eye like a big pizza pie" or even "Shoo fly pie and apple pan dowdy," but we did it on purpose. They seem to do it by accident. So I am delighted with all the progress in record players because a the real value of the new devices is they allow me to listen to "golden oldies," such as "Old Black Magic," to my heart's content.

Tomorrow may be a shocker for today's generation of musicians, as technology and robots replace all but the most talented artists. You may recall that recording devices replaced live musicians in theaters and radio some sixty years ago. Tomorrow's computers will read music, simulate instruments, dub in a voice, and do the mixing itself; practically speaking, it will just need someone to select a song style and turn on the switch.

What the female sex will do in this new age, in which there is no Fabian that they can scream for, still needs to be worked out. But as they say, "You ain't seen nothing yet," so hang on to your oldies, wherever you are. Maybe clear diction, like the South, will rise again.

FRIENDS

Grandpa, did you have lots of good friends?

"A true friend is someone who thinks that you are a good egg, even though he knows you are a little cracked."

—Bernard Meltzer, radio host

1. IT SEEMS LIKE ONLY YESTERDAY

Someone once said that "friend" is one of the biggest words in the dictionary, at least in terms of the influence it has on your life. I am sure we all have examples of friends that helped us succeed, and maybe we picked a bad friend or two along the way and suffered some consequences.

My parents, as long as I can remember, were always cautious about who we played with, labeling some boys as having "bad blood" (whatever that meant). I recall that one of the boys who played on our sandlot baseball team fell into that category. He was a really good ballplayer, so despite his rough style, everyone was anxious to have him on the team and fully expected that he would someday be a high school star. However, he lived on a street where a few fathers were tough guys (read they "served time"), and so their kids acted like they were tough guys as well. The rules of life seem to be that when you act tough, eventually you have to do something tough to support your image, which then leads to tougher stuff and trouble with the law. Our tough young star ended in reform school and never had a chance to excel, giving my mother the chance to use one of her favorite expressions, "You are known by the company you keep!"

Over the years we all have had many friends and relationships, some from the old neighborhoods of our youth, others from a team we played on, a club we enjoyed, a job we worked on together, or simply by chance. Those relationships helped us enjoy life more fully, get other opinions, and may have helped us grow up. A good example of the extra boost you get from a friend came when I was running every day. I found out that having a fellow runner gave me that extra incentive to get out there, as well as to run a little further. In the same way, a friend at work may give you that extra little push to reach a goal, where you might hesitate if you were alone.

When I went to college, I had to work part-time to pay my bills. It was a tough challenge in a demanding school with a lot of homework—a challenge that got me very discouraged. However, in my off-campus job, I became friends with a feisty WWII veteran, Tim McSweeney, who had lost both legs and now worked at the college town's post office. He had a heart of gold and always encouraged me. One day I told him I was thinking of quitting school due to finances and stress. After giving me a coarsely worded, stern lecture on never quitting anything, he got me a job driving a postal truck at night—a job that allowed time for homework and solved my financial stress as well. I have always thought of him as one of my real heroes, one to whom I owe a lifetime debt of gratitude. He was a classic example of the adage that you are only as strong as your friendships.

The most important type of friend is a "best friend." Most of us have found that best friends generally have a number of common interests, hobbies, and goals; have a mutual respect for each other; and enjoy each other's company. Best friends can disagree yet remain good friends, as the other bonds of the relationship are so strong. This type of friendship can build a long-term, healthy relationship. Some last a lifetime, and some do not.

One of my first best friends in early childhood was someone with whom I went camping and played basketball. We generally did everything together, all the way through high school. Upon graduating, we both enlisted in the military, but he had longstanding plans to follow in his dad's footsteps and become a police officer in our hometown, so naturally he joined the Army and the military police, a great decision that carried him through the next thirty years of his life. My goal was to attend college, and that was only possible with a scholarship or the GI Bill. As a result, I enlisted in the Air Force (model planes being one of my hobbies), got trained in this new-fangled thing called electronics, and eventually went off to college and built a very different set of interests, goals, and friends. While we continued to have good wishes for each other, the lack of mutual interests let us drift apart.

I have been lucky and had several "best friends"—guys who I would call when I had great news or a crisis, guys that I could talk to when I messed up and who were so close that they seemed to be one of the family. For example, after high school, when I was trying to decide my future, my uncle strongly urged me to work with him at a large GE factory where I would have some job security. He felt that my family needed income and college was a "waste of time." My mother hoped I would go to college but was concerned with the finances. One of my best friends from childhood advised me to forget my uncle's narrow view and find a way to pay my own way through college. He knew I wanted more out of life than a job and that I longed to travel, and he knew I could do well in school. His logic was that if I failed in school I could then take a job, but if I first took the job, I would never have the opportunity to find out what more I could achieve. He was a perfect example of a best friend being like family—someone who knows the real you. Such friends are few and far between and are a treasure that shapes a lifetime.

Best friends and good friends may change over time, but the importance of friends is a fundamental part of your success throughout life. (Building friendships should be a mandatory course in school.) For example, when I was sixty years old, two long time friends chose me to help solve a huge business problem for them. Because of our friendship, trust and mutual respect, we were able to create one of the most successful new business ventures of my lifetime. The thrill of that success was the result of having strong friendships.

For some lucky people, a spouse is also a best friend, one that has mutual interests beyond just the children. These interests encourage doing things together so that a deep bond can form and strengthen both parties, sometimes creating stronger people than either could have been as individuals. When you see a couple who have been happily married for many years, that is usually the case. After fifty wonderful years, this is something to which I can personally attest.

The lesson learned is that there are all types of friends. The best friends help you build a better life and push you beyond what you would possibly be, if you were all by yourself. Best friends are the most important treasures of a lifetime. There are also close friends that can guide and influence your choices along the bumpy road, through advice or support. There are also friends that can drag you down. So your social choices are important. Basically, friends are the footholds that make climbing a mountain possible. You get them by being their best friend, as well.

2. MY FAVORITE FRIENDS

READER LIST OF FRIENDS WHO MADE A DIFFERENCE

3. TODAY AND TOMORROW

Today, with digitized social networking, the use of the word "friend" is very misleading. The term should be -"acquaintance," indicating that Facebook offers a "nice-to-know-you function" and has little to do with the "art" of having real friends. As we all know, "friendship" is a two-way street that benefits both parties, allows us to share our deepest feelings, helps us realize the value of trust, teaches us to listen rather than talk, and allows us to be "taken down a peg" when we get too self-centered or begin to "believe our own press clippings," so to speak. Social networking provides little, if any, of this help.

The need for best friends and buddies is just as vital today, or maybe even more so, than when we grew up. Kids meet and communicate with more kids with broader backgrounds now than in our day. For example, we went through primary school with the same kids, partially because parents were not mobile, partially because ethnic groups lived together, and mostly because all our activities were local. That made it easier to select and build long-term friendships. Today, mobility and short-term relationships are a way of life.

Grandparents can play an important role in a child's social life, and in fact can be close friends themselves, despite feeling that "we have nothing to talk about" or the kids are "so smart technically, that I am embarrassed to talk to them." Today's kids need a foundation to build upon—people who they know can be trusted, who have their interests at heart, and who will listen and not lecture. They need to know that success in life, just like sports, is based on the fundamentals— in this case, the quality of your friends. I heard an old quote, the author unknown, who summed it up: "True friends are like diamonds, precious and rare; poor friends are like leaves, they are everywhere."

Tomorrow, we will see many changes, but the need for "best friends" is a basic need of human nature. I suspect that there is no replacement for the feeling of being together, one on one, and talking out the big problems of life, sharing moments of laughter, or simply sitting along the bank of an old stream, fishing pole in hand, watching the clouds go by.

Somehow, I do not think that Twittering or sending Facebook information will ever be a viable substitute for a real, live, old-fashioned buddy.

N

WORK AFTER SCHOOL

Grandpa, did you have to work after school?

"If you don't want to work, you have to work to earn enough money so that you won't have to work."

—Ogden Nash

1. IT SEEMS LIKE ONLY YESTERDAY

The old woman at the corner store checked my little muscles and then offered me a nickel a week if each morning I would carry a gallon-bottle of oil up to her pot-bellied heating stove. I was ten years old and a nickel bought a lot of bubble gum, so I entered the job market.

That job did not last long, as another store needed a grocery delivery boy, pulling a red Radio Flyer cart for tips—a job that quickly provided some life lessons about fairness and people's attitudes. For example, I discovered that there was an unwritten rule that the people who live on the highest hill and/or the top floor of a building buy the most groceries, and are invariably the smallest tippers! Who knew? There are probably government studies and advice books on this phenomenon, but I knew a bad deal when I saw it, so I quit and took a morning paper route, using an old, one-gear, fenderless Schwinn bicycle I had rebuilt.

My bike and I picked up seventy-five newspapers at 4:45 a.m. every weekday, folded and spun them onto customers' porches as we rode by, and then dashed home for breakfast and off to school. This worked well all summer and fall, as it did not interfere with school or playing baseball in the afternoon, but then winter came and reality set in. Reality is walking or riding the snowy, frozen hills of a New England town at five in the morning with up to thirty pounds of newspapers, just to earn $3 a week. It is cruel and unusual punishment. Even worse, when I collected from my customers on a cold Saturday morning, some customers didn't tip, or worse, never paid their bill. I knew even at the tender age of thirteen that I needed a new profession, one that was warm in the winter and did not depend on people's generosity.

With that profound knowledge, I applied for a job at the local butcher shop. There I did so well that a year later I was trimming bones, grinding hamburger, and helping make sausages; I became a union apprentice, getting twenty-two cents an hour. I was a real worker! No tips to rely upon, no four a.m. alarm clock, and no snow! Fortunately, I could still play basketball at the recreation hall after dinner, but now my Saturday (a big shopping day) sports were out. The other drawback to being a butcher apprentice was that I learned to never eat sausages again.

Of course, I enjoyed having real money, and Mother even allowed me to buy some of my own clothes for the first time. Was I on a roll! Then I got a call from the local pharmacist, who was looking for a soda jerk. Choosing between making ice cream sodas and making sausage was a no-brainer. The hours and pay were better, and my friends would get extra large sundaes—a sure way to be a very important guy. I soon learned two more lessons: that your business loyalty is to the person who pays you, not to your buddies, and that even being near ice cream is very fattening.

Fortunately for my waistline, a year later the largest grocery store in the area lost its chief clerk; he had enlisted in the Air Force and so the store was looking for someone with experience. To make it even better, I had just turned sixteen. That meant I was offered full wages and some training under an old Irish manager—a savvy old-timer who really knew the grocery business. That job carried me through my junior and senior years of high school, helped pay for a newer Schwinn bicycle, my blue suede shoes, and my team jacket. Interestingly, fifty years later I can still remember the prices of the products that we sold in that old store, products such as coffee, tea, milk, bread, and cheese. We had to memorize those prices back then, as there were no bar codes or electric cash registers. (I can't help shake my head at the prices we pay today.)

I also learned a lot about the dangers of living on credit, because the store manager would provide credit (out of his own pocket) during the week; this helped folks who lived paycheck to paycheck. In most cases, the customers were appreciative and made sure they paid him, but every now and then tragedy struck—severe illness, or a husband blowing the paycheck on horses or booze. Sadly, it was almost always the same people who failed to pay. The financial troubles that people got themselves into served as a rude awakening to a young man, but a valuable lesson in living.

Shortly after high school graduation, I followed in the steps of the prior chief clerk, a boy I had known quite well, and I too enlisted in the Air Force (a best friend inherited my old grocery job). A year later, I accidentally met the store's prior chief clerk, far across the country in Denver, Colorado, where he was now a master sergeant, so he could not spend time with me, a lowly private. However, due to his store training, he now managed the base supply depot; since my background was like his, Air Force life seemed to bode well for me.

What I had learned so far was that whether you worked on a farm, worked as a store clerk, delivered newspapers, or helped paint houses, the benefit of working was feeling that you were becoming your own person—a feeling that built valuable personal confidence, not to mention the fact you could buy those extremely important blue suede shoes that Mother thought were a waste of money.

2. MY JOBS WHEN I WAS YOUNG

MY LIST	READER'S LIST
Grocery deliveries	
Store floor sweeper	
Snow shoveling	
Newspaper deliveries	
Bag boy	
Soda jerk	
Stock boy	
Magazine sales	
Grocery clerk	
Farm chores	
Magazine sales	
Assembly Line	

3. TODAY AND TOMORROW

Today, there are many forces that limit the available work for youth, not the least of which are labor laws, automation, the glut of applicants, and a lack of time. For example, delivery boys with the old Radio Flyer carts used to be in demand when mothers walked to the neighborhood groceries; today, they drive several miles to Costco or other stores for bulk purchases. Furthermore, stores now have to worry about the legal issues if a delivery boy is hurt or worse.

In addition, grocery clerks and baggers are somewhat less in demand due to automated checkout features. But even when those jobs are available, they are filled by a grownup: someone working a second job to make ends meet, a senior in need of a little extra cash, or an experienced worker who was unemployed. In short, there are fewer opportunities for young people to work and learn what it means to "make a living."

Even newspaper delivery requirements have worked against the energetic youngsters. For a delivery boy to make money today requires a large number of customers, all serviced in the wee hours of the morning, and so it therefore requires a van instead of a bicycle. In addition, parental concern for a child's safety usually precludes such a lonely job at that time of day.

Maybe farms are today's last bastions of youthful chores for pay, as despite automation there is still an endless supply of farm work and a shortage of manpower. After all, someone has to "muck out" the cow stalls if we are to have milk. Oh yes, and some farms still need someone to stuff fresh, homemade sausage.

Tomorrow, our children will find after-school jobs even harder to come by; there are simply too many workers and too few jobs. Automation, globalization and legalities are permanently changing the world of work, more than most parents and teachers realize.

But if that is the future, where will kids learn about living? How will kids learn the practical wisdom of providing for oneself, saving for a rainy day, understanding the value of money? I think that applying a little elbow grease at an early age helps one appreciate the practical side of life as well as become educated on why parents cannot and should not afford the latest thingamajig. If money remains an abstract idea until after school days, it is a bit like flunking a course in "living," but graduating with high marks in basket weaving.

I hope the next generation will realize, just as we did, that people don't "find themselves," they "create themselves"— and that real work experience builds your foundation. The other reason for early work is, as my mother said, "Idle hands and idle minds are the devil's playground." Now that I look back at it, she sure was right—again.

0

COMMUNICATION

Grandpa, did you use Twitter?

"Whoever said that things have to be useful?"

—Evan Williams, Twitter co-founder

1. IT SEEMS LIKE ONLY YESTERDAY

In the old days, my grandfather refused to have a phone in the house, feeling that if he had anything to say to someone he wanted to "see their eyes"; this was a grumpy position, which he eventually lost to my grandmother's more practical need for gossip. In those days of high-priced long-distance calls, all her gossip was local, simply because so few members of the family or even friends moved very far from home. Far off friends were contacted by mail, written in cursive, costing a mere three cents, arriving three or four days after it was posted, and, hopefully, replied to a few weeks after the original missive had been sent. During this period, the telegram also had its heyday, as it was electrically sent and delivered relatively quickly by bicycle, at less cost than a phone call. Interestingly, telegrams used code words to keep down the length of the message, as the number of characters determined the price that Western Union charged. (It appears that some Twitter abbreviations today had their origins in the dark, distant, yellow-paged telegrams.)

At my uncle and aunt's farm in New Hampshire, which was located miles outside the nearest town, they had a "party line," one line which any neighboring farmer might also use. They had that system as late as the 1950s, because the cost of running updated telephone lines to the back country was so high. When their old farm phone rang with two long and two short bells, it was usually someone calling my aunt; any other pattern of bells was for one of the neighbors. However, a person who was a true gossip or "busybody" would pick up the phone and listen, no matter whose ring it was, just to be "in the know." Of course, the local switchboard operator could listen to all the calls, so she knew everything that was going on in town (and sometimes was the equivalent of a local "Wikileaks").

The other source of information, the US Postal Service, was the best in the world for secure, dependable, private delivery, so it became the preferred source of communicating with family and friends. The postman, despite rain, snow, or sleet, also delivered the Sears and Roebuck Catalog, a tome of over a hundred avidly read pages covering all life's needs. I suppose mail order from Sears was a precursor to Amazon, albeit a slow one.

A big communications change occurred in our lifetime. The 1950s and 1960s were the age of mobile families, where company transfers separated us from good friends and family. That meant that contacts with many neighborhood friends were soon relegated to a once-a-year Christmas card list. This mobility changed how folks communicated and to a great extent ruptured the ideal tightly knit families and neighborhoods that had built the country. "Growing up" in the future would lack many of the role models that channeled and tamed our energies.

Fortunately, advances in communications made dramatic improvements in both cost and effectiveness; this helped folks "stay in touch." The long distance call rates (which had strained marital relations at times) dropped dramatically due to computerized central switches, so mothers were free to gossip and exchange family information across the country, if necessary. (However, some fathers, especially those with daughters, still placed an egg timer near the phone as a reminder to "cut it short.")

Hidden from view in the 1930s, the seeds of Twitter and Facebook were planted in the form of ham radio and walkie-talkies; both types of devices became essential during the war years. Ham radio sets had been around since the late 1920s. Some folks who loved tinkering with old radios (or crystal sets) eventually got an FCC license and set up clunky shortwave sets in their homes. They would spend all evening communicating with like-minded folks from around the world (sounds like an email pioneer). These ham sets had made great progress in size and power in the '30s and '40s, but my uncle's old set was still big, clunky, unreliable, static-filled and costly; nonetheless, it gave him the freedom to talk (gossip) long distances basically for free.

The walkie-talkie and mobile radio innovations, which had been utilized by our troops for short-distance messages, needed devices that could fit in trucks and cars, and this eventually gave birth to the CB radios. The term "breaker, breaker" signaled that someone in a truck or car wanted to break in on a trucker's conversation; a handle or moniker ("This is the Big Dog calling") was used to hide real identities, and "good buddy" was a term used for folks you never saw, all of which laid the ground work for new approaches in the future—the phenomenon we now call cell phones.

Other new communications technologies allowed AT&T (the only telephone company back then) to replace the local operators with switchboards and direct dialing. The wooden, wall-mounted telephone in our home was made obsolete by plastic handsets, mostly made by Western Electric. The "dial zero" and "Information, Please" operators were replaced by 411 and 911, and the unique party-line bell rings became ten-digit numbers. (By the way, Americans complained that no one wanted to remember all those numbers. AT&T ignored that advice and succeeded. This inspired the government to introduce zip codes for mail years later.) At that point, we had much smaller phones that could dial to anywhere in the world, with better clarity at a lower cost. Who could ask for anything more?

But progress never sleeps and soon we had the incredible cell phone, which has more features than anyone can remember or need, in a package that is so small I need my glasses to see who is calling. An ancient Greek philosopher said, "There is nothing new under the sun," but I would have to add, "But that doesn't stop engineers from repackaging it."

2. MEANS OF COMMUNICATION I REMEMBER

MY LIST	READER'S LIST
Party lines	
Crank handle phones	
Operator, long distance please	
Direct dialing	
Wlkie-Talkies	
Western Union boys	
Singing telegram	
Switchboard operators	
Sears catalogs	
Three cent stamps	
WWII V-mail envelopes	
Princess phones	
Glass line insulators	
Ham call letters	
Special delivery letters	

3. TODAY AND TOMORROW

Today, I cannot imagine what my grandfather, who wanted to "see someone's eyes when he talked," would think of our communication systems. Would he think that Skype counted?

Today we have everyone instantly and simultaneously available at all times, in any and all places on earth. The new interconnected world of Twitter and Facebook takes gossip and the old "party line" to a new level of urgency, insisting that everyone stay in touch and relate their every waking thought and action to as many people as possible. In this new world, we replaced "busybodies" with hackers, crank calls with advertisements, and privacy with identity theft; all trade-offs that may make you wonder. Personally, if anyone invades my privacy, I think they should be forced to use a crank phone for life.

In my perspective, this endless need for faster communications has a big downside; everything has become too small. Telephone screens require reading glasses to see the numbers, mini-keyboards defy my stubby fingers, and the copious extra features are too confusing and mostly irrelevant (although they are the ones the local salesperson assures me that I cannot live without and which, incidentally, add many dollars to my phone bill). My not-so-unbiased opinion is that there should be laws that make twelve-point font mandatory for all devices and dictate that phones have fewer features than a computer.

Tomorrow, communications may offer Skype-like holograms so you can project yourself as a 3D image into a friend's room and have an intimate discussion—or even be counted "present" for a class. You, in the meantime, can stay at home and twitter with everyone in the remote room. This all may excite our grandchildren, but I agree with that old sage Shakespeare, who might have said, "Twittering is much ado about nothing".

Frankly, I would still prefer to pour two tall, cool beers, open a bag of peanuts, kick back in a lawn chair, look a man straight in the eye, and discuss whether the Red Sox will rebound from another disappointing year and win the Series next year. That is a heart-to-heart discussion, not a phone call or Twitter message. Grandpa might have been old-fashioned, but knew what he was talking about.

SAYINGS

Grandpa, what were your favorite words and sayings?

"I really didn't say everything I said."

—Yogi Berra

1. IT SEEMS LIKE ONLY YESTERDAY

It seems that every generation has a list of new words and sayings that they own, hoping, I guess, to make their generation unique in history, or at least to befuddle their parents and teachers into thinking so. These special sayings and words seem to declare that this is a new era, one where the old rules no longer hold, where only we young people can "dig it" and older folk are "square" and need to "chill out."

Of course, we now know that fooling our parents with fake words was just "rattling their cage" and while we might have thought we were the "cat's meow" at the time, we were really still "cruisin' for a bruising" and had yet to "face the music"; eventually we would have to bring home the "bread." Father, who thought all young people had "bats in their belfry," had no hesitancy in ignoring our "jive" and informing us that we did not know "diddlysquat" or "beans" about life. We knew better, being "cool," but he had us "over a barrel" as he had all the "moolah" for gas. We also "got a grip" on the fact that if he "went ape" we got a kick in the "wazoo" and were "grounded," ruining plans to go to the "passion pit" on Saturday night. So, despite different "in words" we still communicated.

That is not to say that my parents and grandparents didn't have their own sayings and special words, just as we did. Some of their words stayed in use for several decades, even though they lost all connection with the original meaning of the expression. For example, "easy as falling off a log" was originally about the way lumberjacks risked falling into the water during a logjam, but in everyday usage it meant easy to accomplish. In many cases, we understood what the expression meant, but if you were just learning English, you couldn't possibly guess the connection between the words in the saying and the original intent.

My parents used expressions such as "talking turkey," which we know means "being direct and to the point," but turkeys do not talk and are in no way direct, even when faced with the axe at Thanksgiving! My folks also loved to use the term "hogwash," meaning that a recent alibi or excuse we had made up was unbelievable; but hogs rarely wash, as can be attested by anyone who has visited a pig farm, so why this expression? If our excuses were only somewhat unbelievable, they would say, "poppycock," though where it came from and why it was less stern than "hogwash" was never explained. I will leave it you to figure out "horse feathers."

We also got in trouble if we "played hooky," something that would draw severe punishment from parents, teachers, truant officers, or all the above; these folks all clearly understood the term, yet what was "hooky"? I did read an explanation that hooky had to do with going fishing, rather than attending classes, but that may be just "a line." (Ouch)

Another such term was "riding the gravy train," which meant having an easy job that paid well; but again, what was a gravy train? Assume you had a friend visiting from a foreign country; would they visualize a railroad tank car being filled with gravy from the Sunday dinner and then offering rides? My parents also used the term "he has an axe to grind" as a way to say someone has a personal motive, or "living on the razor's edge" for someone who lives dangerously, expressions that defied literal translation but became common usage. Also, a "high mucky-muck" was a very important or pompous person, but you could only translate that if you were from the Chinook Indian tribe, it seems.

Some other terms were so hard to explain that they would give a translator the "heebie-jeebies." If someone died, they were said to have "kicked the bucket"—presumably the one under the cow, but what the cow had to do with anything remains a mystery. Another great example is the term "saved by the bell," a term eventually used to define a boxer who was knocked down and would not have gotten up if the end of the round had not occurred. However, the term was originally used in the graveyard, where so many folks were literally buried alive (by accident) that coffins were equipped with a string that attached to an above-ground bell, and which people, upon waking and finding themslves in a coffin, would pull. The caretaker on the "graveyard shift" (another term that evolved) would hopefully hear and dig them out. Thus they were "saved by the bell."

Grandmothers would say, "Be good, for goodness' sake," or "Do something for goodness' sake," emphasizing that the basis for our actions should be goodness, I guess. Another, "Land sakes alive," which was a gentle way to say they were surprised, originally came from a seaman's expression, used after long months at sea, expressing surprise they were still alive when they first saw land. The expression "when my ship comes in" had a similar origin, as seamen only got paid after they docked and sold their catch; but that evolved to mean "when my luck changes, everything will be better."

My generation's words and sayings seem to have been influenced more by girls, cars, entertainers, and WWII than by the farmers and sailors who influenced my parent's era—a not-so-surprising result of more people having an urban lifestyle, and the new influence of radio, early TV, and movies.

In high school, for example, let's say you noticed a friend, a "cool cat," who had a "ducktail (or DA) haircut," at the "passion pit," where he was "making out" with a good-looking "bobbysoxer" in his "hopped-up wheels," which "bummed you out" because you had tried to date the "chick," who you thought was "the most," but you had been "shot down" despite your "cool" pegged pants, knit tie, and blue suede shoes. So when you saw your friend and he asked, "What's buzzin' cousin?", you simply said, "Later, gator!" and "split." Not much of the farm or sea influence on these sayings!

It seems that kids have always had their own language, and parents have always rolled their eyes.

2. MY FAVORITE SAYINGS

MY LIST	READER'S LIST
Parents and Grandparents List	
Land sakes alive!; Goodness sakes!	
Saints preserve us!	
My stars!; Egad!	
When my ship comes in	
On cloud nine	
Fit as a fiddle	
The gravy train	
Nothing to be sneezed at	
Up to snuff	
Hogwash, poppycock, horse feathers	
Left-handed compliment	
Going off half cocked	
Went to pot	
Lock, stock, and barrel	
Chicken feed	
My Generation	
Can you dig it?	
Hep cat	
He's square	
Wasted	
It's a gas	

Burn rubber	
Life of Reilly	
Right on!	
Daddy-O	
Far out, man!	
Outta sight!	
Hubba-hubba!	

3. TODAY AND TOMORROW

Today, most seniors are pretty square when it comes to kid's slang expressions; parents are not very "hep" either, and kids still like it that way, despite living in a more dangerous world. The slang and expressions still come from music, which now includes rap, and is also influenced by TV and digital games, as by liberal entertainment venues. And, of course, it is spread very easily by Twitter.

Some modern kids' sayings are just simple fun, such as "bling" for glittery jewelry, "kicks" for shoes, "'rents" for parents, "glomp" for a big hug, or "Yo, what's up?" which replaced our "Give me five." In addition, we have an entire new Twitter language that, like the old telegrams, limits the number of letters per message and by necessity creates short-hand words that creep into the language. Some are easy, such as fab, fav or OMG. But "LOL" does not mean "lots of love"; rather, it translates to "laugh out loud." "IMHO" means "in my humble opinion", and "Twead" means to read a tweet or twitter message. Dig it? If you took time to twead, you would wonder whether future kids would ever be able to write a real letter—a question I am sure my parents also asked, but for different reasons.

However, most of the new slang is beyond my interest (just like mine was to my parents), and so I find it easier to insist, as my grumpy uncle once said to me, "Speak English when you talk to me. I don't speak gibberish."

Tomorrow's kids will invent more new slang and sayings, but hopefully our computers and cell phones, which already come equipped with automatic foreign language translation, can add "slang translation" as well. Maybe then we can be part of the modern conversation. I hope so, because 60 years of slang has sure taken its toll on me.

WHAT WILL I BE WHEN I GROW UP?

Grandpa, did you know what you wanted to be when you grew up?

"Anything in life is possible, if _you_ make it happen."

—Jack LaLanne, fitness guru

1. IT SEEMS LIKE ONLY YESTERDAY

We were children of "Depression parents," folks who grew up when jobs were scarce, when welfare was almost nonexistent, when there were no unemployment benefits and no social security or pensions, and when workers saw no promise of better times ahead. Then, to add to the misery, WWII and rationing made food, fuel, and clothing even harder to come by. During that period of turmoil, the American Dream that had lured immigrants to the United States seemed doomed, and millions of people returned to their roots in Europe and Mexico. It was a time dominated by thoughts of survival, not of planning a future career.

Naturally, this time of uncertainty and parental struggle influenced a young man's dreams about what he should do when he grew up. For example, my grandmother had seen her hometown burn to the ground, then she moved to the States, only to experience the Great Depression. She was determined that her boys were going to have a better life than their parents and that meant having job security, insurance, your own home, and an affordable lifestyle. Security for her boys meant jobs with the government—which she knew from experience had never had a Depression and always made its payroll. Her boys could choose to be policemen, firemen, or postal workers, but they were government-bound and she brooked no discussion; she owned the dream. Only one son challenged that dream, and he became a bank vice-president, only to be told by Grandmother that he had not succeeded like his postal superintendent brother. (To some extent, that perspective proved to be correct, as the American economy has had recessions almost every ten years since FDR.)

By the early 1940s, however, there were plenty of temporary "war effort" jobs, if you were willing to relocate. Many folks left their old lives behind them and went to the Kaiser shipyards in California or to Detroit, where Ford automobile plants were building jeeps and tanks, and further West to build the Boeing B-29. During those two decades, the 1930s and 1940s, peopled focused on getting a job—any job in any place that supported the basic need for food and shelter.

Fortunately for me, in the late '40s and early '50s, jobs were becoming more plentiful, FDR's social security programs eased some of my parents' fears of the future, and some of the boom from the war years carried forward. New technologies, ones that evolved from the war, created entire new industries and a huge demand for skilled workers. Companies began to offer pensions just to attract workers, and worker unions won better job protection and wages. "The times they were a-changing."

That good news meant that we were allowed to dream a little more and a little bigger; the bad news was that there were so many possibilities it made our heads swim. I can recall my fickle thoughts after a Saturday matinee, when I was sure I wanted to be a cowboy; then on Sunday I visited my uncle's fire station, saw men sliding down the neat brass pole, leap into their fire gear, and dash down the street with blaring sirens, and suddenly that seemed to be the perfect job. A few days later, I might have seen *South Pacific* and been swayed by the Navy's bell-bottom trousers and exotic adventures to the Pacific Islands, or maybe I had just watched Ted Williams hit one over the Fenway fences and decided to be a ballplayer.

My book-reading habits were also an influence, especially those books about nature, ones that complemented my scouting. They made me think about a job as a forest ranger. (The fact that I had never been in a real national park did not seem to deter me.) The world had gone from no opportunities to too many possibilities in a little over a decade.

Reality set in after high school graduation. Suddenly I realized that I did not have as much control or independence as I thought. Neither was I quite the "gift to the world" that Mother kept telling me I was. Even worse, parents, generally, were fed up with feeding and clothing a growing boy, and the growing boy was chafing under parental rules, so that led me to one conclusion: I needed a self-supporting job of any kind. For me, there were only three options: get a job at a local business or with the government (most of my relatives favored this latter option), go to college (my mother's fondest hope, despite a lack of finances), or enlist in the military.

Timing, as I would continue to learn throughout life, is everything. In this case, the Korean War started, opening up a new but unplanned for solution. By enlisting, I would immediately be out of the house and on my own, would have a chance to learn a skill (and, as I found out, some discipline), and best of all would be eligible for the GI Bill; the bill offered a partial scholarship, making college affordable for me. Finally, being in the service gave me more time to decide what I really wanted to be when I really grew up. That plan and timing turned out to be the winner. It worked out (unlike most of my plans) even better than I had hoped, and put me on the track for a career in the newly emerging computer industry. Mother could not have asked for more.

So, the answer is no, I did not know what I wanted to be when I grew up until I actually grew up. But I sure had a lot of fun thinking about the possibilities.

2. INFLUENCES ON WHAT I WANTED TO BE WHEN I GREW UP

MY LIST	READER'S LIST
The Depression and economy	
Military	
Grandparents	
Parents	
Teachers	
Father's example	
Movies	
Books	
Events of the time	
Siblings	
Best friends	
Heroes	
Unemployment	

3. TODAY AND TOMORROW

Today, this age-old question still persists. "What will I be when I grow up?" A youth yearns to know where they are going and wonders if they are somehow, even a little bit, in control of our own destiny. Many of the same influences we knew, maybe in greater or lesser amounts, are still there, shaping young people's thoughts and interests. After trying fortunetellers, Tarot cards, palmistry, and tealeaves, I concluded that tomorrow is just an ever-expanding today. In other words, making the most of today creates your future.

Grandchildren still want to hit the baseball like a star; only the hero's name has changed from Joe DiMaggio to Alex Rodriguez. They still dream about playing professional football, but want to pass like Tom Brady rather than Joe Montana. Or maybe they prefer a career as a golfer like Phil Mickelson, having forgotten about (or never having followed) Sam Snead. All those possibilities are more real today than ever before in history, as are incredible business opportunities and personal independence.

However, today's children face some new obstacles, ones we never knew, and those obstacles make planning ahead even more difficult for them. For example, their tenth grade computer studies will be obsolete by the time they graduate. The same can be said for the fields of medicine, construction, and even transportation. The speed of change is far greater than anything we had to deal with and shows no sign of slowing down, which makes planning what to do when you grow up very difficult for a young person. One thing is certain: having solid fundamental skills to build upon is no longer a luxury; it is mandatory. "Study now, play later" is today's motto.

To make planning a future even more difficult, there is a deep skepticism about the integrity and values of industry, banking, and government, a feeling that makes any life plan very difficult. These issues were around in the Depression years as well, but had been resolved or hidden pretty well until the '80s. I imagine that time will correct the problems again, but in the meantime Grandpa's influence and inspiration is needed, at least as a cheerleader. Someone needs to counter all the negative stuff and over-expectations. Someone has to help sort out the meaning of all these changes. After all, Grandpa has seen most of it before.

On the plus side, today's kids have access to far more information about more subjects than was available in our formative years—or if it was available back then, it was not in a form that we could access with the click of a button. Theoretically, this explosion of knowledge should help children make more educated decisions about what they like and what they really want to be when they grow up.

Tomorrow, however, is more uncertain than any time I know of. As Yogi Berra said, "Predicting is very hard to do, especially about the future." In our world of tomorrow, local influences will give way to global relationships and more automation, creating new opportunities and dissolving old traditional ones. Young people will, once again, find themselves seizing any opportunity to support themselves, and the "dream jobs" will be few and far between. Due to all that change, we may find that social work, trades, and government jobs are the predominant careers in our society. I hope we will not come full circle to my grandmother's wisdom, where a government job is the only dream.

SECTION 3

Now That You Are Older

"One day you will see that it all has finally come together.
What you have always wished for has finally come to be. You
will look back and laugh at what has passed and you will ask
yourself, 'How did I get through all of that?'"

— Author unknown

W hile that great quote is not always true, it is the hope
we all harbor, as we grow older. "How did I get through
all of that?" is a question I often ask myself, with some level
of amazement! Things happen to us, things happen because
of us, and things happen despite us. But when you look back
and add up all the peaks and the valleys, all the sorrows and
the joys, the love and the pain, then you realize how special
the journey has really been.

All the joy and pain of growing up, layered onto our lives
year by year, helped prepare us for the "big time," the challenges of dealing with family, homes, careers, military, personal adventures, and most of all coping with the moving
target that we call life.

Life, as we learned, is full of surprises, some good, some bad, and a few that actually worked out the way we thought. The ones I enjoyed were the ones that engaged my entire being, generated a passionate experience, and left me with memories and friends too dear to ever lose. As Tennessee Williams wrote, "Life is all memory except for the one present moment that goes by so quick you can hardly catch it going." That is to say that our lives are a collection of special moments in time, each stored safely in our memories.

In the following pages, I have chosen some subjects that evoked strong memories of the adult years and used examples of some of my special moments. I think most of us tend to best recall special memories that answer the question I raised earlier, "How did I ever get through that?" I also assume that my grandchildren or friends might read my book, and I have made an attempt to avoid mixing memories and too much imagination—imagination being a tempting enhancement to any memory.

If you enjoy the topics I have chosen, then add your own moments, and if I missed a topic, add your own pages. After all, as I said earlier, the joy of life is that each life is unique; the sad thing is when those unique memories are simply lost in the mists of time.

AUTOMOBILES

Grandpa, what were your favorite automobiles?

"If I'd asked my customers what they wanted, they'd have said a faster horse."

—**Henry Ford**

1. IT SEEMS LIKE ONLY YESTERDAY

People often said that the automobile replaced the horse in terms of men's affections. This affection for automobiles, however, was practical and had little to do with beauty. For example, the disappearance of "Dobbin" made our streets a whole lot cleaner and less aromatic, as well as safe from horseflies. (That is a big deal, if you recall those days of yore.) The automobile also eliminated the tasks of mucking out the horse barn, oiling the harnesses, and wielding the curry brush. Automobiles did not bite, kick, or step on your foot. Folks seem to forget those little details.

Another big advantage of the automobile was that it allowed folks to move to the suburbs and even commute from the country. This was a far-reaching change, as, prior to the car, city folks had been forced to live near work or make many connections on trolley, bus, or rail services. For example, before I had a car, I took a trolley to the subway station, and after a twenty-minute ride I took another trolley ten minutes so I could walk another ten minutes to get to work. That was a pretty typical commute, and one that made cities very crowded.

My uncle bought the family's first car, a 1935 Ford coupe with an 85HP motor, running boards, moleskin seats, and three-speed manual shift, because he had a long trip to work and, as a fireman, was always on call for emergencies. The fact that he loved tinkering, loved driving the ladies, and became our favorite uncle when we rode in the rumble seat, had nothing to do with his buying a car, of course.

The original heavy, steel-bodied, black cars of the 1930s and 1940s had few options in design, color, or function. However, about four million of them sold in the United States in 1940. (Production of cars stopped in 1942 entirely, due to the war, and did not get back to any big redesigns until around 1948 or 1950, when Detroit built six million cars.)

Even so, some of the emotional and romantic attachment to cars—the "horse syndrome"—lingered on, so a young man's first car was a big milestone in his life—almost bigger than getting his first long pants. However, with gasoline at twenty cents a gallon, homes having one-car garages, and parents' abhorring debt, car ownership, for most folks, was a grown-up luxury until well into the 1950s.

My first car, one I earned after I had graduated from high school, was a green 1947 Mercury Coupe, which I got for the princely sum of $150, due to the fact it already had thirty thousand miles on it, which in those days was a lot of wear and tear. No matter. I used my small pay to personalize my "steed" with fender skirts, whitewalls, a windshield visor, a "suicide knob" on the wheel, and pine incense on the dash. Every Saturday, I carefully simonized the car (which seemed to remove a lot of paint for a so-so shine), a ritual for my drive-in movie date. What I soon discovered was that a car, much like a date, costs more than you had planned. I also discovered that the winter moisture and salt on the road had attacked the floorboards of the car, a rust attack that even the thick metal used in that time period could not deal with. In addition, my Mercury burned a quart of oil per thousand miles, and gas had jumped in price to twenty-five cents a gallon! Plainly, this car was a high price for mobility. Fortunately, Uncle Sam needed me and I had to sell the car, albeit at a loss of ten whole dollars. Repair costs were the first of many automobile lessons that I learned the hard way. (By the way, there were no costs of car insurance policies, warranties, auto taxes, or inspections.)

I learned another car lesson when I drove a home-modified, fifteen-year-old 1937 Ford in a stock car race. It was a very exciting hobby, until the mechanical brakes failed and instead of joining the other cars making the turn I continued by myself, straight ahead, soaring up over the bails of hay that lined the track and landing in a crumpled heap, very embarrassed. I had learned that dangerous sports are for the professionals and that I should stick to safer hobbies.

Beginning in the mid '50s, the national highways were expanded (thanks to Ike's national highway bill), local roads became smoother, long-distance driving increased, automobiles got more reliable, and Detroit got style-conscious. Tail fins, fancy taillights, two-tone paint, vinyl leather upholstery, and enormous motors were the hallmarks of Detroit's golden age. The Olds 88, Ford Thunderbird, Lincoln Continental, Nash Ambassador, Studebaker Commander (by an Indiana firm that had been around making buggies and wagons originally), and the Packard Caribbean all resembled luxury yachts, albeit on land. It was an exciting time for car buffs, and men's affection for automobiles was at its peak.

The side-effects of the automobile are a tale of massive culture creep. Initially, it simply meant building a few more roads, bridges and tunnels. But the more they built the more people drove, and the automobile finally gave birth to endless traffic and parking problems. The new suburban living, which the auto made possible, also led to "shopping malls"—a new revolution in marketing. (Without the automobile, there would be no Wal-Mart or Costco, for example.) Another side effect combined the back seat of the car and the new rage, the drive-in movie. This combination was accused of corrupting the morals of young people, who could easily escape parental oversight. Even worse, the automobile made fast food restaurants practical. And finally, the automobile was the source of a great deal of personal and (future) national debt, as well as a gobbler of oil resources. The lessons learned here were "there is definitely no free lunch" and "every change has unintended consequences that you may not like."

By the 1950s, young men dreamed of sports cars, something flashy, preferably convertible, with mufflers that made folks know you were coming and attracted pretty girls whose hair blew in the breeze as you drove along—a sports car that looked just like my used, red Austin-Healy. My sports car taught me a few more "car things": (1) s lot of girls don't like to get their hair mussed up by the wind, despite what the movies show; (2) Old English sports cars require tune-ups every weekend at a minimum; (3) bucket seats were not made for long drives or necking; (4) rough roads and low-slung cars do not like each other; and (5) generally speaking, inexpensive, used, foreign cars are actually very expensive.

Finally, I graduated from college and got a real job, so I naturally needed a real car, just as my uncle had years before. My two-tone green 1956 Ford Fairlane had a continental kit (spare tire kit) on the rear end, whitewall tires, fender skirts, and enough chrome to outshine the sun. The car also needed constant care, of course. My Ford was the source of many arguments with my friends, who were General Motors fans and felt Ford's products always "nickel-and-dimed you to death with small repair needs." (These brand loyalty arguments were just as fervent as today's PC-versus-Macintosh debates.) Fortunately for me, my new boss, drove a Lincoln, so I was on the side of the angels. However, I did get a lot of body rust and learned how to patch holes.

But it was near the end of an era, an era where we had once repaired our own cars, fine-tuned the engines, customized the design, and made the car feel uniquely our own. After the '70s, cars became over-engineered, with tremendous horsepower and electronics, and repairs required computer diagnosis, which ended the personal touch that had made cars so special. The same was true of design. For example, the 1956 Ford Thunderbird was one of the all-time great small car designs, but the engineers kept making it bigger each year, until finally it was just another car with no personality. This loss of romance (horse sense?) in Detroit, plus increasing costs, opened the market, first for Volkswagen and then for Nissan, Toyota and Honda. Detroit engineers focused on size and glitz and left the less profitable market to others, thereby opening a Pandora's box of foreign competitors. Detroit responded with the under-engineered, unreliable Pinto and Corvair small cars, but it was too little, too late.

I must grudgingly admit that the foreign cars were more reliable, lasted for far more miles, and did not require so much manual labor and simonizing on the weekend. However, they rarely had the same personal attraction as an old classic Mustang, or for that matter, the emotional attachment of the old horse the Mustang had replaced.

2. MY FAVORITE AUTOMOBILE MEMORIES

MY LIST	READER'S LIST
Johnny/suicide knob	
Fender skirts	
Moon hub caps	
False whitewalls	
Dual mufflers/pipes	
Four on the floor	
Hood ornaments	
Tail fins	
Running boards	
"Souped-up" engines	
Double clutching	
Inner tubes	
40-weight Penn State oil	
Clean and gap spark plugs	
Starter button	
Stripped gears	
Crankcase	
Chopped and lowered	

Leaded gasoline for 29 cents
Mechanical brakes
Bondo Dent Repair

3. TODAY AND TOMORROW

Today we seem to have too much of a good thing. From the country's economic success and population growth came time-destroying automobile commutes, as well as the terrible loss of life and property from accidents, air pollution, unsustainable use of natural resources, and even worse, a situation where one-quarter of our suburbs and city's real estate areas are now given over to roads and parking facilities. In addition, we now have cars that talk to us, instructing us on where to turn and even how to park! Worse, to build enough cars to meet demand, the automobile industry now designs cookie-cutter cars, which lack the graceful lines, artistic touches, and individuality we saw before and shortly after the war years. The old Cord, Jaguar, DeLorean, Ford T-bird, Lincoln Continental, and Corvette are still among my favorite designs.

Then there is the cost issue. Gasoline, like any commodity in short supply, has gone from twenty cents when I was a boy to roughly four dollars a gallon in 2011. If that is not enough add in the cost of insurance, inspections, and property taxes, or the unbelievable repair cost of a simple fender bender. The only virtue of a new car is reliability.

Today, almost everything, from delivering food to the store to getting to work to taking kids to school, depends on trucks and cars. The oil barons applaud our progress. I guess we gave up the horse and created a monster that we cannot live with or without.

Tomorrow, I have to believe that we will see solutions to many of today's issues, as our country is too creative to endure these problems much longer. Furthermore, the staggering increase in the use of automobiles in Asian and South American countries should create the funds to invent major changes, hopefully in conjunction with US firms. The trend, due to concerns about emissions, will be toward much lighter vehicles made with new metals. These smaller cars will alleviate parking issues, as well.

The most far-out driving concept that I have seen is an electric car that you do not drive, but rather simply punch in your destination in the dashboard and you are driven to your destination point under satellite and Google-maps control. This avoids getting lost, road rage, and most accidents, and supposedly provides a precise commute time, during which you can read the newspaper. Now, if they can only add chrome, fender skirts and dual mufflers!!

Now that I think about it, maybe the days when we had to clean out the old horse stalls weren't so bad after all!

S

JOBS

Grandpa, what were the jobs you liked best?

The only job where you start at the top is digging a hole.

—Anonymous

1. IT SEEMS LIKE ONLY YESTERDAY

Enjoying your work is a rather recent idea. For example, my grandfather, who went to the Grand Banks on fishing trawlers, got caught in the middle of a winter gale, watched his ship get crushed by the ice packs and then sink into the depths. He survived, left the sea, and came to the United States where he became an ironworker, trading the danger of the ship's rigging for the girders of new skyscrapers, steeples, and industrial chimneys. In both cases, he took pride in doing a "man's job," but I doubt that he would say that he "enjoyed" his working conditions or called it a career.

In the early 1940s, one of our neighbors, whose firm had failed in the depression, had to take a job with the WPA to "make ends meet." This was FDR's "Works Program Administration," a part of the New Deal that created jobs to rebuild roads and parks in an attempt to boost the economy. My "white-collar" neighbor certainly did not enjoy his work. In addition, I know that my father, after the frightening days of the Depression, appreciated the security and stability of his postal work, but I think he "enjoyed" the fact that his family was cared for more than the actual work. My uncle liked the income and prestige of working in a bank, but hated the tedium of paperwork. But most people felt lucky to have any work at all, as many did not.

My mother, once my father died, had to support three kids on her own. There was no welfare in those days, except emergency medical help for kids. So she bought the corner grocery store as a way to have income and still be close by her children. Mother had been a stay-at-home mom who had expected to cook, sew, crochet, and knit, not to go to work. She had no retail experience, was a fairly shy person, and hated haggling. But as she often said, you do what you have to do when times are tough. While she did not like the job, she got her larger wish: all three kids finished college.

In the '30s and '40s, any jobs that were available had many applicants, and therefore employers had no need to make jobs enjoyable in order to entice or keep workers. If you didn't like the job, they had plenty of applicants who would step in and who might even work for less money. (Sound familiar?) Many business owners and financial magnates were characterized as greedy, self-interested, and ruthless; it was the age-old conflict of bosses trying to get as much as possible out of each worker for the least cost, and workers giving only as little as necessary for as much as they could get. Roosevelt and then Truman enacted legislation and regulation that curbed excesses and took a position that industry had a responsibility to the 185 million people who then lived in our country. In other words, business success was a national priority, but it was not an end unto itself. FDR had a lot of opposition to this position, but by curbing excesses, he had built the foundation for decades of future prosperity. The lesson learned one more time, as it had been throughout history, was that success for both labor and management depends on carefully caring for the golden goose, not greedily killing it.

When I was young, the work we did was so different that my grandkids think I am a Martian invader if I mention this stuff. For example, any typing you did was on machines that went clackety-clack and ping. A mistake meant pulling the paper out of the typewriter and doing it over. If you wanted a copy of the page you inserted a sheet of carbon paper or made a mimeograph master and cranked (literally) out the number you needed. We used mechanical tabulators, as calculators had no electric models until the late '50s, never mind battery-powered units. In place of the hand calculator we had slide rules. Adding up a bunch of numbers on a piece of paper was an expected skill for many jobs. A cash register was just that: key in the total, listen to a whir of gears, watch the drawer open and then factor the change yourself. At the end of the day, you reconciled the sales slips, cash in the drawer, and the beginning balance—all by hand. No bar codes identifying the purchased item, no price look-up except in your own memory, and no credit cards at all! How's that for revolutionary?

Even the tools were different back then. We drilled a hole with a brace and bit and elbow grease. We smoothed off a board's edge with a hand plane, sanded it down with a rasp, cut it to length with a crosscut hand saw, and used a claw hammer to nail it in place. Elbow grease!

Until the 60s, there were no commercial computers, a program was something you got when you went to a concert, software was not even a word in the dictionary, Bill Gates had just been born, and Diners Club's new credit card was just beginning to be accepted in restaurants. In other words, we actually did all the work ourselves.

However, our generation got lucky. The United States workplace was already disrupted by the enormous effort of WWII and the Korean War, so it was ready for all the changes the new discoveries brought about. The war funded a lot of creative energy designed to improve everything from food to transportation to bridge building. Suddenly, jobs became plentiful because the new technologies from the war had created entirely new high-skilled industries. Jobs that had once required muscle had suddenly been made obsolete by automated manufacturing techniques for tanks, planes, roads, and foods to fight the war. Many machine tool inventions, new communication devices, and transportation improvements, ones that might have taken normal business decades to enact, were forced into place by the government. Some incredible new products were a direct result of the war: radar gave us the microwave oven, jet planes replaced the slow propeller-driven models, synthetic rubber replaced the vulcanized rubber tires of the past, and dried foods and frozen foods replaced canned goods (and even fresh produce) as new refrigerated trucks made markets accessible to remote farms. Clothing took advantage of the new nylon fibers used in the war years and launched wrinkle-free cloth. By 1950, our generation had entered an entirely new world, one driven primarily by technology!

The speed of progress between the '60s and the '80s broke both the sound and the sanity barrier. The biggest leap was the commercialization of computers. The first computers I worked on in the '60s used reels of magnetic tape (instead of DVDs) that were read by machines the size of a man; the printers, which were black-and-white text only, were as large as desks. The computer required huge cables and air-conditioned rooms (the air-conditioning units alone were as big as automobiles), so the building which housed them usually required full-time maintenance men. One customer bought an IBM 360 Model 75 for five million dollars, and that system had far less capability than today's $500 iPad from Apple.

Due to all this change, employers and employees were faced with a new balance of power, one where men (and women) had choices of jobs, especially the new, more complex jobs that actually required training and turned employees into company assets rather than replaceable commodities. When the war ended, millions of people were returning home looking for work. The government created the GI Bill, which subsidized all levels of training to support these new inventions, and that educated labor force gave birth to the employment boom of the 1960s. It was an era when the new, more mobile American society, created by the war, was ready to jump at new opportunities.

Of course, some lucky folks understood what they really liked in life and went after it. For example, a friend of mine who enjoyed detail and structure became a CPA and loved his work, finding that his orderly approach to things helped many people. Another friend's father was an engineer, and the son followed in his father's footsteps, eventually enjoying the creation of dams and bridges that protected folks from floods they had endured for decades. And yet another, who loved the outdoors and animals and would have been miserable in the first two jobs, chose to become a farm manager. For those who enjoyed engineering and applied themselves, there was limitless work. Suddenly, many regular folks could choose to work at jobs they enjoyed and make a good living— maybe for the first time in history.

My grandfather once told me that if I did not make a good living, I would be miserable, but if I made too good a living, I would be even more miserable. The goal, he felt, was to be in the middle, doing something you enjoyed. He was a sage old guy, my grandpa. My high school counselor, a Mr. Curnane, told me that if I did not enjoy my work, I would have an unhappy life, so I should choose wisely. They must have met!

So, with that background, let's go back to my grandchild's question: "What were the jobs you enjoyed and why did you enjoy them?"

For me, the fun in any job was being allowed to use my creativity, overcome difficulties, and make new things happen. Part of that "can do" feeling came from growing up in our era, a time when you personally had to solve problems to survive. Some of my friends preferred less challenging work, leaving them more time for other family and non-work activities, but I enjoyed working. But still, it is a frightening question for a youth, "What work makes you happy, and what bad choices will make you unhappy?"

As an example of a bad choice, I took a job as an apprentice steamfitter, working on heating and cooling systems at Harvard University (a job that punched a hole in my exalted view of Harvard students). After finishing training, an apprentice typically got the late-night emergency calls no one else wanted. One night, the Harvard Medical School morgue called complaining that the cooling system had sprung a leak, and my boss said that I was the obvious choice to go fix it. When I got there about two a.m., a little, wizened, old caretaker let me in and escorted me through a deathly quiet room full of white-sheet-covered tables, to the area of the leaking pipe joint. Just as I reached for my wrench, one of the sheets rose up and then it lay back down again! Of course, my terror rose up and <u>did not</u> come down again. I screamed. The little caretaker giggled. He then explained that there is always air in a dead body and it sometimes moves, causing a limb or body to lift momentarily. Who knew? Despite his explanation, I fixed that leak in record time. I had already decided this was the wrong career for me, and this incident just helped me leave it faster.

The computer industry, on the other hand, I found very appealing. It was a pioneering environment that required personal creativity to find better ways of doing things, and it helped people in other fields do their work better. It turned out that the rapid changes in technology also meant there were new creative opportunities every year. It was like a having a grown-up's sand box full of toys to play with. The frosting on the cake for me was that the firm I worked for had such a high level of integrity and offered great benefits. (Best of all, it had no morgue.) This time I had made a good choice for a career.

One example of a job that I found enjoyable was being a manager, but many people dislike that role. The pleasure I got came from helping people develop their skills and careers, improve their own goals, and strengthen their personal lives and fortunes. As many managers know, when one of your staff goes on to achieve great things, it really makes your work enjoyable. That is especially true in sales management, where you can inspire people to reach seemingly unreachable goals. However, when someone fails at his or her job, it may lead to the unpleasant responsibility of parting ways with an employee, often one you had tried to "save." Unless you have a thick skin, each one of those occasions is very painful.

I suppose that is why one of my oldest friends, a man who had been the firm's star salesman for many years, refused any promotions to a management job, because he knew he could not fire an employee, no matter what the reason. He knew himself well, and worked at what he enjoyed doing—working with customers. He once said that life was a much shorter trip than any of us think, and that enjoying your family and your work and helping a few people are the only important stops on that highway. Similarly, my mother had a cross-stitched, framed saying on the wall that read, "Let me live in a house by the side of the road and be a friend to man." As you can see, greed was not in vogue.

So my most enjoyable work was on projects that enabled me to help people succeed, play with new technical gizmos, solve problems, read, and write, while at the same time limiting the things I disliked, such as repetitive tasks or being a hard-nosed manager. (And I purposefully avoided anything to do with biology and sinking ships.)

The value and problems of work are really important things for grandchildren to understand. As usual, it is the small details that distinguish success from mediocrity, and pleasure from boredom. Those little things such as timeliness, dependability, preparation, integrity and stick-to-itiveness— all things that are important in sports, by the way—make a big difference in achieving career success and satisfaction. Here is a great place for grandfather's to provide stories that show the way.

2. WHAT MADE WORK ENJOYABLE

MY LIST	READER'S LIST
People you work with	
Opportunity to grow	
Interesting projects	
Solving problems	
Not boring	
Work to be proud of	
Team work	
Meaningful solutions/products	
Security	
Respect for employees	
Good pay	
Location	

3. TODAY AND TOMORROW

Today, looking back, I think that people my age were truly fortunate and lived in a golden age. During our working years, we had the highest level of job security in history; some of us worked for the same firm for several decades. In many cases, we worked for firms that had noble goals and ethical standards, and which produced useful things, thereby providing real job satisfaction. We were also the first generations to retire well; pensions, social security and health insurance made being older a better experience than any other generation had enjoyed in history.

I am optimistic that those great days will return, but in the meantime, it appears that we are in a period of adjusting to the forces of automation and globalization, which are disrupting the number of jobs that are available, as well as the skills that employers need. These severe labor market changes are not new and are always unpleasant. After the Korean War, for example, the emphasis in industry shifted from mechanical engineering to electronics engineering. Mechanical engineers either retrained or lost their earning power. Other labor disruptions happened when automatic tabulators displaced many bookkeepers and automated phone systems replaced telephone operators—all requiring personal adjustments for job seekers.

The 1970s and '80s each had serious recessions and workplace turmoil. But in each case the ingenuity of the American people created new industries, such as the space program, computers, and new construction. This led to new and exciting careers for those that could adjust to the times, and serious problems for those that did not.

As Henry Ford said, "There is a subtle danger in a man thinking that he is 'fixed' for life. It indicates that the next jolt of the wheel of progress is going to fling him off." This is all too true.

Tomorrow, as I see it, our grandchildren may get lucky, just as we were. Once again, we hope to have entirely new industries develop based on nanotechnology and biotechnology, paving the way for new ideas that will transform the ways most things are manufactured, revolutionize medicine, modernize our transportation, help the environment, and change the entire field of energy. Much of today's knowledge will become obsolete (again), but learning new things will be much easier and quicker over the Internet. This need for fast-changing education will probably revolutionize our education system as well. In other words, from the ashes of today's problems we will see the birth of a new, exciting era of opportunity for our grandchildren, just as new opportunities defined our own lives.

There is an old saying that nothing is certain in this world but death and taxes. But we now know that the other certainty is "change," so our grandchildren will require the same adaptability and flexibility that we needed. They will cope with new jobs, new skills, new lifestyles, and even new places to work, just as we did. Henry Ford's quotation will apply to them as well. In fact, adaptability may be even more important to them, as the speed of progress seems to be accelerating.

I have faith in this new generation's adaptability. I think that anyone who can learn to type with only his or her thumbs should be able to adapt to anything.

GREATEST ADVENTURES

Grandpa, what were your greatest adventures?

*"When I used to read fairy tales, I fancied that kind of thing
(adventures) never happened, and now here I am
in the middle of one!"*

—Alice in Alice's Adventures in Wonderland

1. IT SEEMS LIKE ONLY YESTERDAY

Everything seemed to foster a spirit of adventure in my lifetime, a spirit informed by tales of our relatives braving the stormy Atlantic Ocean in a flimsy wooden ship to come to a country they had never seen. They learned a language they had never known, ate foods they had never tasted, and risked all they owned in order to find a better way of life than they knew in the teeming, disease-filled cities of 17th-century Europe.

In addition to our parents' and grandparents' exciting stories, books such as Mark Twain's *Adventures of Tom Sawyer* and the *Adventures of Huckleberry Finn* made us think of floating down the Mississippi, books about Davy Crockett's harrowing escapes on the wild frontier inspired ideas of camping, and Edgar Rice Burroughs' *Tarzan of the Apes* glamorized how we could survive the dangers of the jungle and be a hero at the same time.

Through movies that showed us the space travels of Buck Rogers, or Captain Nemo's submarine diving through perils at 20,000 leagues under the sea, Hollywood alerted our generation to the fact that science was the new opportunity for adventure. Both of these fictional adventures seemed unbelievable at the time. But eventually they became reality, as we watched the U.S. Navy nuclear submarines sail under the North Pole in 1958 and NASA make the first moon landing in 1969.

WWII and the conflict in Korea had also fanned the adventurous spirit by forcibly taking young men, who in some cases had never been outside their home state, and making them world travelers. These travels often launched adventures fraught with mystery, high risk, and discovery. The Navy advertised, "Join the Navy and see the world," and the Marines sang about the exotic "Halls of Montezuma and the shores of Tripoli" to appeal to the adventurous. Movies and music focused on fascinating places, individual heroics, and mystery. *Anchors Aweigh* with Frank Sinatra and Gene Kelly,

Casablanca with Humphrey Bogart and Ingrid Bergman, and *South Pacific* with Ezio Pinza and Mary Martin made staying home seem pretty tame.

Of course there are other types of adventure, which are risky and exciting but not in the ways that wandering through a jungle in Borneo or sailing solo across the Pacific are. It takes a spirit of adventure to start a new business, bet all your assets and reputation on the unknown, accept risks beyond your control and willingly face disastrous consequences, to find a pot of gold. Similarly, it's adventurous to give up a secure job and take the risk of a new start, or to give up a simple life to take on a challenge that will make life better for your family. Almost everyone has know adventures like these, which proves that all adventure is not physical—unless you count the resultant ulcers.

When I look in my rearview mirror, which I am allowed to do at this age, I can see many of my small adventures that were part of growing up. Some of them felt as traumatic (if not as dramatic) as meeting an elephant in the jungle. Many of us can recall the first day we went to school, an apocalyptic day when we felt torn from Mother for the first time, utterly alone, facing the unknown jungle of rooms and hallways, the frightening, albeit smiling face of a teacher, and the stark fear that we would never see home again. For some of us, we had a similar feeling the first time we had to give a talk, sing a solo, go to a dance, interview for a job, or attempt a myriad of other learning experiences—all of which combined enough mystery, fear, and newness to be classified as personal adventures.

In addition, we all have the unplanned adventures, frightening or at least risky events that take us by surprise. For example, I was doing an every-morning, boring chore of cleaning out my family's small, three-cow milking barn when suddenly a neighbor's large, amorous bull came through the doorway. I was standing between him and our cows, one of which I guess he felt was particularly attractive, and the quiet morning was suddenly filled with snorting, stamping, and mooing. I had never realized until that moment how Spiderman climbs walls, but pure adrenaline is a wonderful thing. It got me up into the hayloft and out of harm's way in one leap! Then there was the time our ferry got caught in a hurricane off the coast of Nova Scotia...but that is a story for another time.

Clearly, "adventure" is a personal thing, one that gets redefined based on the time and place of the adventure and is customized by your personality. But any event that gets the heart racing and the adrenaline flowing is just as much an adventure as one that gets you glory.

One glamorous adventure—one that I suppose was inspired by Tarzan movies—was a safari that I went on in Kenya. I enjoyed the people and the country, but when you are that close to the raw power of nature, when you can literally taste the danger, it gives you a very different perspective on what is important in your life. When you are in the cage of a Jeep and the lions and water buffalo are roaming free, you appreciate the dangers that our ancestors faced. When you see a cheetah bring down an antelope, you realize that we do not write the rules of life, Mother Nature does. In my case, I stood breathless as a rhino the size of a Sherman tank debated whether to charge our group. Unforgettable!

However, my best adventure was one that mirrored my ancestors' adventures, in a way. This adventure took me across the wide expanse of the Pacific Ocean (rather than the Atlantic, which my ancestors crossed) to a land I had never seen, where I had to learn a new language to get by, to do a job whose success was very much at risk, and finally, where food supplies were plentiful but quite different. My new adventure was in Japan, as opposed to my ancestors' New England, and the challenge I faced was not fighting the elements, but competing with the dragons of the Japanese computer industry. I learned another lesson, one my parents knew: adaptation and flexibility are basic survival skills of every adventurer, no matter the time period, location, and nature of the risk. A Japanese proverb for this is, "The bamboo that bends in the wind is stronger than the majestic but rigid oak."

Any overseas business assignment is truly a wonderful adventure—some locations riskier than others—but in my case, the challenge and mystery of learning Asian cultures, adapting to their foods, working with their customs and politics, and learning their belief system was an adventure that changed this adventurer's life forever. I found that international adventure reshapes one's perspective about the world, one's country, and oneself. Every young man should try it—assuming that they are willing to eat something besides chicken nuggets and live without a Starbucks coffee.

2. MY ADVENTURES

MY LIST	READER'S LIST
First day of school	
First big job	
Joining the Air Force	
Visiting New York City alone	
Working overseas	
Starting a new business	
Safari in Kenya	
Climbing in Nepal	
Climbing Mount Fuji	
Whitewater rafting in New Zealand	
Flying in a glider	
Scuba diving	

3. TODAY AND TOMORROW

Today, due to the wonderful adventures by explorers and scientists in the 20th century, we lifted the veil of secrecy that surrounded exotic places, plants, animals, and peoples all around the world. We also have the benefit of photographic and video adventurers preserving the stories of virtually every unique place, tribe, or landscape, and posting it so we can all enjoy these discoveries conveniently from the comfort of our homes.

While there is still much that we do not know or appreciate, we have made great strides in the past few generations. Sixty years ago, when I graduated from high school, if someone had said that I would make a two-day round-trip to Japan, explore the hinterlands of Burma, or fish in Costa Rica, I would have thought they were crazy. Unbelievable changes have happened in just a few decades.

Today, I suppose that the Internet reduces some of today's travel mystery and quantifies some of the risk—at least on our planet. After all, I can go online to Google and look up the Yak and Yeti Hotel in Nepal, or "where to eat in Myanmar." That takes some of the old mystique out of trial-and-error traveling. That does not mean that there are no great adventures left, as a climb in the Himalayas or diving off the Great Barrier Reef is still a heart-stopping experience. In addition, travels in some parts of the world are still fraught with danger (although more from other humans now than from wild beasts), and the adventures of a new business or great research project can still turn a young man's hair prematurely gray. Adventure is still there for the adventurous.

Tomorrow, our grandchildren will have adventures beyond what we dream of today, eventually searching through the stars, plumbing the ocean's depths, and pioneering entirely new approaches to medicine and government. That era will be fraught with new mysteries and new dangers. But that is what our grandchildren's lives are supposed to be about. Or, as Eleanor Roosevelt once said, "the purpose of life, after all, is to live it, to taste experience to the utmost, to reach out eagerly and without fear for newer and richer experiences." We had our day, and now our grandchildren can stand on our shoulders and take their turn reaching for the stars. Mr. Spock, where are you?

HOMES

Grandpa, what were your favorite homes?

"Be it ever so humble, there is no place like home.

—**J.H.Payne**

1. IT SEEMS LIKE ONLY YESTERDAY

Think of an attic filled with old trunks of yesterday's treasures, a parlor cupboard with shoeboxes of once-precious photos, a cellar workbench with old tools and drawers of "things I may need someday," a dining room cabinet of Sunday-best china stamped "made in England," a bedroom blanket chest with grandmother's handmade afghans and quilts, a bedroom toy box where old teddy bears and Lincoln logs still wait to be played with, an old kitchen filled with the smells of baking bread, and a living room with lace doilies and needle point creations decorating an old player piano, and you have my description of my that wonderful word, "home."

Of course, some of the words that described everyday things in my old home are rarely used or needed anymore. A word like "piazza" has been replaced with the more mundane "porch," for example. And some features we knew have disappeared as well, such as the cellar coal bin, the woodshed, the root cellar, pot-bellied stoves, the ash barrel, the coal furnace, the kitchen stove's chimney damper, the wooden match box, the ice chest, the clothes wringer, the scrubbing board, wooden clothespins, brass water pipes, and, very thankfully, the outhouse.

In my uncle's farmhouse in New Hampshire, which he built himself, he incorporated the outhouse into the back hall, right next to the woodshed, to save everyone the great distress of going outdoors in the middle of winter. However, the farmhouse only had a huge kitchen wood stove as its "central heat" source—meaning that, theoretically, heat rose from the first floor through grates in the ceiling to reach the bedrooms—but there were no vents to the ice cold back hall. This heating design created two rules of life: the first was to never get up in the middle of the night to go to the outhouse, no matter how great the need, and the second was that at bedtime you put on your pajamas in front of the stove then ran upstairs and dove into the goose-down bed and comforters, vowing not to move again until the stove was refueled in the morning. Fortunately, my uncle added some wood to the stove before he began milking at four thirty in the morning! My uncle explained that it was more pleasant in the barn at that time of day, due to the warmth that the draft horses and cows generated, but I never bothered to find out if that was true. However, no matter how cold it was, I was certain to get up for a breakfast of homemade bread with jam from big preserve jars, thick creamy milk and fresh eggs, all prepared on a giant wood stove.

My grandmother's home in the city (actually a "flat", as fewer people owned their own homes back then) was not only warmer, but had no outhouse. The cast-iron radiators that warmed each room received noisy hot water from a coal furnace in the cellar; the furnace was fed coal several times a day, banked at night, and cleaned of ashes each day. At the end of the week, the heavy ash residue from the coal went into barrels, which were rolled out for town waste collectors (unless it snowed, and then the ashes were applied to the sidewalks and stairs). Grandma's indoor flush toilet was a major technology breakthrough, one that had been introduced in the U.S. shortly before 1900; it became one of those absolutely essential features that we now take for granted. The combination of these "modern" conveniences, plus Grandma's tasty cooking, made her house my favorite.

As an added treat, after church each Sunday, we would walk to Grandma's house and float up the stairs on the aromas of fresh bread, pot roast, and pies. The tantalizing scents created sufficient incentive to put us on our best behavior, such as following orders to clean our plates, keep our elbows off the table, chew our food, and remember that children are to be seen and not heard. Despite the discipline, it still seems that her meals, prepared on an old, black, gas stove in heavy cast-iron pots, were some of the best meals I have ever eaten. Her good food and tradition made other relatives come as well, and after Sunday dinner Grandma would read their "fortunes" in their leftover tea leaves—a fortune that invariably had a ship coming in and never seemed to have bad news. When the tea leaves conversation began, my grandfather and the menfolk would retire to the den where Grandpa would sit in his favorite chair, smoke his pipe with Prince Albert tobacco, and regale us with stories of his adventures at sea until he quietly fell asleep, leaving us to go play before going home.

My family home was a small bungalow (another outdated word)—a home that would have been too small as the family grew up, but benefited from my other grandfather's carpentry skills, as he and my father added on two unfinished upstairs bedrooms (and a storage area); one was Grandpa's sleeping quarters and the other was for my brother and me. Our joy at having our own rooms was a bit tempered in the summer, due to poor insulation for the roof (it was before the joys of air conditioning), which led to sweaty sheets, hot pillowcases, and little sleep. Fortunately, my father also added a screened sleeping piazza or porch, overlooking our backyard's homemade swings and horseshoe pit. The piazza provided a cool breeze and night sounds, a treat that seemed like a real camping-out adventure.

The other cool spot was the cellar. It was a damp, dark place of spiders and who knows what else. There was a bench and a set of shelves used to store winter vegetables and preserves such as jams, jellies, pickles, and tomatoes (which occasionally exploded from fermentation and made an awful mess), and sometimes there was homemade root beer and sarsaparilla. The cellar also had a coal bin, a wooden enclosure where the coal truck made deliveries during the winter, noisily tumbling coal down a long metal chute, causing soot to fly everywhere. But in summer, the bin stood empty.

The favorite room in the house was the living room, because that was the location of our big radio, in front of which we kids gathered nearly every afternoon before dinner to listen to our favorite adventures. This was followed by some family games or reading. It was there we assembled our armies of toy soldiers, ran our Lionel trains, and practiced our music, and where Mother entertained neighbors and friends.

There are long-forgotten items from home that are still tucked away in my memory. I recall my father shaving in the morning using a straight razor, a strop for honing the razor, and a soap dish and soft brush to lather his face. Once in a while he would go to the barbershop and get a "real" shave, one where they would put a hot towel on his face to soften his beard and end the shave with a splash of Bay Rum. I also recall the old galvanized pails used for washing everything from feet to clothes, the clothesline pulleys in the backyard, the old claw-foot bathtub for our Saturday scrubbings, the old green wicker rocking chair that my grandfather went miles in every day, the great lilac bushes, and the rain drumming on the tin roof of our one-car garage.

Of course, my favorite homes, the richest in love, are those where my own children grew up. These all have special memories, such as building cellar playrooms; creating sandboxes, ice rinks, and tree houses in the backyard; decorating bedrooms so they were fun places to sleep; and, of course, after my hot attic childhood, making sure all the bedrooms had air-conditioning. Today, our attic storeroom is full of old teddy bears, books by Dr. Seuss, an old sled, and boxes we have not opened for years. We live many miles from our original home, but one thing has not changed: home claims a piece of your heart, forever.

2. MY LIST OF HOME MEMORIES

MY LIST	READER'S LIST
Attic clutter	
Cellar storage	
Tin-roofed garages	
Bedroom summer nights	
Living room radio	
Dining room china	
Kitchen cooking	
Home furnace	
Old wash tubs	
Hanging out the wash	
Ice boxes	
Home-made linens	

3. TODAY AND TOMORROW

Today, "home" is still a word that makes even grown men teary-eyed. It may have become even more important in our current, rootless world, and yet also harder to define. The strength of the word as we knew it came from the memories that seeped into the very walls of the old homestead. Home also came with a network of relatives and neighbors that supported us when we failed and applauded us when we triumphed. It was our haven in the storms of life, a magical, healing place to return to from a bad day playing ball, unpleasant duties in the military, or unhappy days in a marriage.

However, in the past several decades our society has become nomadic, wandering to wherever a job takes us or fleeing to better weather down South, and forgoing the network of supportive relatives and neighbors and the stability of lifelong friends. Some folks move multiple times, cleaning out closets and attics as they go, and losing some childhood treasures. In addition, where we once received just a few gifts, such as a single teddy bear, we are now rabid consumers with lots and lots of stuff, making attachments to things more diluted and old treasures less magnetic. All this seems to make "home" a more difficult concept, and is one more reason that the solid rock of grandparents' memories are a critical foundation for family roots.

Tomorrow, if nomadic trends continue, home will literally be where the heart is and won't have any relationship to solid walls. Maybe a new RoboDog will replace the century-old Teddy Bear; Red Ryder's BB gun will be reengineered into a rocket launcher; and an iPhone game will replace the family Parcheesi board. Maybe Facebook and a network of online friends will be as supportive as daily face-to-face contact of old neighborhoods. Maybe Google will help guide and support young folks through life. I doubt it, but maybe.

Whatever happens, life will be a lot emptier if there is no concept called "my favorite home."

V

MILITARY

Grandpa did you like being in the Air Force?

"Why don't we just buy one airplane and let the pilots take turns flying it."

—Calvin Coolidge, complaining about a War Department request to buy more aircraft.

1. IT SEEMS LIKE ONLY YESTERDAY

When I was ready to graduate from high school, the country had just finished winning a war against several bullies (Hitler, Mussolini, and Tojo) that had threatened to take over the world. Our fathers and uncles had come home from the war with stories that were both exciting and frightening, and the movies were full of patriotic feelings and romantic impressions of war. And yet we knew the story was not over, as Russian and Chinese communism posed yet another threat to the world. The threat of an atomic war made everyone realize how fragile our lives were and how vulnerable the country had become.

With all that turmoil, it was difficult for me to see what the future would bring. I had no real idea of what I wanted to do with my life, had no money to do anything with it anyway, and had always enjoyed model planes, so I decided that the Air Force would be an exciting place to spend a few years. I was in for quite a shock—some of those jolts would be for the better and some for the worse, but they were painful regardless.

Before joining the Air Force, my friends and I were used to (and took for granted, I might add) all the support and tolerance that a mother and father's love provides their children. We seemed to feel that we were entitled to have our bed made, have our clothes picked up and washed, have meals we liked, be gently awakened in the morning, have boo-boos kissed, and so on. We also enjoyed wearing some stylish clothes that made us feel a bit unique, customizing our slicked-back hairstyles, sleeping until ten a.m. on Saturday mornings, hanging out on the corner with the guys, staying up until all hours—in other words, being the normal useless teenagers.

Upon my arrival at boot camp, where I suppose I expected to be welcomed with open arms, I was immediately directed to the barber shop and I recall thinking that it was nice that they liked my carefully combed, Brylcreem locks. I also recall telling the barber not to take too much off the sides, at which he smiled, turned on his shears, and gave me a "GI crew-cut." I was panic-stricken, feeling that no girl would ever look at me again! Strangely, no one in the Air Force seemed to care how I felt. The sergeant then marched about twenty of us down to a tent where a row of medics waited; I naïvely supposed they were going to check us out for our free health care plan. After the haircut episode, I thought I might tell them about some fictitious medical problem I had, get sent home, regrow my hair, and join the Navy. But no, the medics simply formed two rows, like a gauntlet, each with a box of needles, and as we walked through they gave us eight injections—four in each arm—for everything from malaria to malingering. Of course, I had made it more traumatic for myself by staying at the end of the line, hoping, I guess, that they would run out of needles, but inadvertently forcing myself to watch all those needles go in nineteen other arms, with some of their owners dropping in a dead faint. Somehow I survived all that abuse and headed to get a new uniform, but I was not a happy camper.

Now I had seen the very stylish, tailored gabardine uniforms of the enlistment officers, as well as one worn by an officer who lived in our hometown, but to my surprise we only got two sets of drab khaki fatigues, klutzy brogans, and even worse underwear (known as "skivvies"). The clerk allowed, with a snicker, that they were all the clothes that we would need for several weeks. Fortunately, they gave us a fatigue hat, which covered my embarrassing baldness. We were then told to send our civilian clothes home (including my blue suede shoes), as there was no room for them. It was a true statement, as our only storage space, a full-sized footlocker (obviously, also khaki-colored), could barely hold our fatigues and skivvies. That was the last straw. I told the sergeant that I thought I had made a mistake and would rather go home; he nicely explained that I had signed a contract, and that Uncle Sam owned me for the next four years, so I should get with the program. I did not sleep well that night, and it got worse when we fell out for five a.m. reveille—a time that was closer to when I used to go to bed, not get up—and then, for some perverted reason, did calisthenics until breakfast.

After pushups, we marched, sort of, to the mess hall, where I learned that later in the week we would take our turn at KP (kitchen police) duty, starting at four a.m. in order to help get chow ready for general mess call at five thirty. Me, peeling potatoes! Imagine! With that lovely morning thought, we continued through the chow line for breakfast. I felt sure that the four a.m. risers were trying to get even with us by creating chipped beef on toast that was so salty it made your tongue sting, oatmeal whose lumps defied chewing, and coffee that was so strong it required corrosion-resistant mugs to avoid springing leaks. A self-inflicted gunshot wound began to seem appealing!

When I first decided to go into the Air Force, a guy named General Hap Arnold had just won a battle to change the name from the Army Air Force to the U.S. Air Force, which among other things meant changing from drab khaki uniforms into the new Air Force blue—a major victory from my point of view. However, they had not had time to change from Army basic training methods, so we got the whole infantry training package. We had an endless litany of orders: making your bed so tightly they could bounce a quarter on it, rolling and storing your clothes in precise parts of the footlocker, cleaning and ironing your clothes so the creases looked like they could cut bread, shining your boots so officers could see themselves in them, etc. And the instructors had rather blunt ways of motivating you to follow these orders. If you chose not to oblige any of these small requests, you had the option of a week's

KP, latrine duty, a ten-mile hike, or midnight watch. Those options were, I was told, part of our education. However, I could not recall my recruitment sergeant mentioning any of this type of education. An oversight, I guess.

I did not appreciate until later that these tough rules and tough leaders were there to save my life and the lives of my group in combat or in an emergency; we were all dependent on the predictable actions of our fellow soldiers. Neither did I realize that they were making a man out of me: forcing me to accept responsibility for myself, changing my personal standards so there was no such thing as "good enough," encouraging self-respect in my appearance and behavior, and teaching me how to deal in the real world (a world where I was not sheltered by my family). They did the job better than most parents could do, as no sentimental barriers softened their choice of words. In fact, I doubt that my mother ever knew that some of the words the sergeant used even existed.

We learned many useful skills, all done according to SOPs (standard operating procedures), which covered everything from how to tie your shoes to how to breathe. For example, everyone had to do exercises before breakfast, hike so many miles a week, have a haircut on a certain schedule (whether needed or not), have square corners on your bed, wear uniforms a certain way, and field strip a cigarette (whether you smoked or not). We all had rifles, which we carried around and around; field stripped, cleaned, and reassembled; and carried around some more, although we only used special rifles for target practice. As we learned, it takes rules and obedience to run a big organization and ensure everyone's safety.

However, the saluting rituals and demands for respect got carried away at times. There was the story of an officer who asked a soldier for a light. The soldier said, "Sure, buddy." The officer then sternly said, "That is no way to address an officer.

Now, soldier, do you have a light?" The soldier snapped to attention, saluted, and answered, "No sir, sorry sir."

Finally, basic training was over. We were issued our new Air Force blues, a real snappy uniform. My hair had grown back, but into a crew cut. And our family was allowed to come and visit us with boxes of goodies. We also got a one-day pass to go downtown, and despite the fact that we were in Ithaca, New York, in the frigid month of March, we fully appreciated freedom for the first time in our lives. It was, however, a short-lived freedom, as the next day we were herded onto a train (a strange way for an airman to travel, it seemed) to go to our next base and back to school again. I thought graduating high school ended my days in classes and I was ready for "real life," so here was another shock. Learning is a lifetime thing! Who knew?

Once again, I benefited more than I expected, as the training was in a field I enjoyed, was led by professors from USC and civilian contractors, and was very complete. Years before, when I was trying to sell enough magazines to win a bicycle, I had enjoyed articles about new technology and making things, so when I took the Air Force aptitude tests, I scored very high in a critical area that was key to engineering aptitude. The newest thing in the early 1950s was airborne radar, and, lucky for me, there was a real shortage for support personnel, which meant openings in basic electronic engineering classes. Those classes applied to my time in the service as well as my life beyond it. (Ironically, I had never sold enough magazines to win the bicycle, but the effort had paid off with a bigger prize.)

There were a lot of other lessons to learn as well, some good and some bad. As you might expect, living in an open barracks with twenty to thirty other men provided a quick lesson in how others define morals, ethics, and behavior; how to cope with those differences in order to survive; and how your "street smarts" that worked so well at home did not cut it in this league. Also, outside the barracks you learned to follow orders and take guff from people who had more stripes or rank than you did, whether you respected them or not—a hard lesson to learn. You also learned that large organizations are terribly disorganized, insensitive, and illogical. Like all the other lessons, this helped in everyday life, specifically when I worked in big business.

But while I was in the service, communism became a clear threat and there was a strong feeling that our country desperately needed us, so military personnel had plenty of support and opportunity. This made up for organizational shortcomings.

It is no exaggeration to say that war is hell and rarely has any redeeming value, but that is the part of history that people seem to forget. If you watch the horror of Ken Burns' documentaries, or movies such as *Saving Private Ryan* or even *Thirty Minutes Over Tokyo*, you would think war would be obsolete by now. If those films do not convince you of the insanity of war, then you should make a visit to a Veteran's Administration hospital and see the real damage a war leaves behind. We owe everything we have to those who served up front.

Anyway, to make a long story short, two years later I was in a nasty plane accident that ended my Air Force career. But like many of my fellow enlistees I took the knowledge I had gained, made use of the GI Bill, earned a degree, and got a real job. (Look Mom, I am finally self-supporting!)

So while I poke fun at some of the crazy days in the Air Force and choose not to talk about some of the bad ones, I never forget all the good my military service did for me. For there is no question that I am a better person in many ways for having served my country.

2. MY MEMORIES OF MILITARY TERMINOLOGY

MY LIST	READER'S LIST
TDY (temporary duty)	
SOP (standard operating procedure)	
AWOL (absent without leave)	
SOS (corned beef on toast)	
Stars and Stripes newspaper	
Sick bay	
Three-day pass	
General orders	
Fifty mission crush (cap)	
Mickey operator (radar navigator)	
G.I. Party (cleaning barracks)	
Gig line (shirt, belt, fly alignment)	
Shoe clerk (a desk jockey)	
The head (latrine)	
Egg beater (helicopter)	
Fruit salad (medals)	
SAC (Strategic Air Command)	
RNAV (radar navigation)	
SA-16 (air rescue craft)	
BOQ (bachelor officers quarters)	
Slicker (con artist)	

There is room at the back of the book to add your special service memories. There is no one else to tell them, so please don't let those moments disappear.

3. TODAY AND TOMORROW

Today, I would guess that computers control everything in the military (although I suppose the brass have kept KP the way it was, just so they have a good way to teach everyone to follow orders). I notice that they still have the fifteen-mile hike and calisthenics in full field pack, but I find it hard to believe they still field strip and reassemble their weapons, because the trusty old M-1 rifle that I used has taken on the look of something from Star Wars. (The old M-1 cost less than $100, but today's M-110 may be over $30,000.) In addition, laser sights and heat-seeking bullets made obsolete the hours we spent on the rifle range getting a steady hand.

The old prop planes that we loved are long gone, but my favorite, the old P-38 Lightning, still compares surprisingly well in speed and range with today's F-35 Lightning jet fighter. However, the P-38 falls far short of the F-35 in terms of payload, armor, navigation, communications, and firing effectiveness. But of course, we must remember that our old P-38 Lightning cost about $100,000, while the new F-35 Lightning costs about $150 million.

The radar technology I worked on was based on a WWII invention that had originally stopped the German Blitz on England, helped destroy the German U-boats which preyed on convoys, and improved strategic planning with better weather knowledge. Today, further advances have brought the military new and almost unbelievable navigation and firing systems, in smaller and smaller packages that can reach targets across the globe.

Today and tomorrow, I suppose one can greet those military and societal advances in science with open arms, or one can regret the loss of the human touch, much as one can regret losing the "feel of the road" that we had in a non-power-steering, clutch-driven transmission, personally tuned, cars of old.

The same is true in military aviation, where much of the "feeling" is gone. In place of "hands-on" combat, dogfights, and bombing, the military weapons can now hit targets around the world, sighted down the radio waves of a satellite by a desk jockey, who has no human touch or personal involvement at all. The impersonal decision maker sees life as a character on a screen, an unreal object, and unemotionally taps the "trigger." That is both good and bad, I suppose.

Tomorrow, will we reach a point where there will be no need for manned bombers at all, just satellite-guided missiles? Will aircraft carriers become obsolete or simply carry drones? Will it be our robots versus their robots, instead of foot soldiers? Will that possibility be scary enough to make war obsolete? If so, will barracks life and the lessons we learned there be mothballed in a museum alongside a P-40 Thunderbolt?

Maybe science will lead us to an impasse and end war. But if so then we need some new way to teach kids to take responsibility for hanging up their own clothes, making their own beds, having a tidy room, and staying in shape. After all, mothers simply cannot say, "Your room is a mess. Get down on the floor and give me twenty push ups. Do it now, #@!@#!" And if not Mom, who will?

GRANDMA

Grandpa, how did you and grandma meet?

*"Sometimes, life connects the dots by happy,
unexplainable accidents."*

—Anonymous

1. IT SEEMS LIKE ONLY YESTERDAY

I think the story of meeting my wife, like many love stories, is best described by the word "serendipity." But let me go back a bit and explain why. Both of my grandmothers either believed in (or thought it unwise to ignore) the power of fate, predestination, the alignment of our stars, or tea leaves to determine one's future life, including to whom and how happily you would marry.

The use of fortunetellers, astrologists, swamis, and superstitions were all part of their era. Today, our science-based culture discards those theories and instead of chance tries to model a person's future with computer programs and dating services. Who is right? I will tell you our story, and you can decide which theory you think might be correct.

My future bride was working in New York City for a large international firm, a job she knew about only because a friend's father had encouraged her to join his division. When the recession of 1960 hurt the funding for her department, she knew she would soon be transferred somewhere else. By chance, a friend of hers was getting married in Boston, and she attended the ceremony, where she happened to meet two old school friends of hers who had just lost their roommate. They suggested that she ask for a transfer to Boston and room with them. Luckily, the firm's Boston office just happened to have an opening for an instructor. She took the job with mystical timing, as it was just before I, unsuspectingly, had enrolled for a class in her specialty.

I had joined this firm solely based on a research project that, luckily, I had done for extra credit while attending a university that this firm just happened to hold in high regard. I was only attending that school because the school encouraged veterans with the GI Bill. They also gave credit for courses that I had taken in the service, which, in turn, shortened the time it took me to graduate; all of those factors had determined the date that I joined the new firm. Interestingly, I had almost transferred schools and had almost chosen to work for a different firm; either decision would have meant that I might never have met my wife.

In another "just happened by chance" occurrence, when I joined the firm, I had nearly gone to work in the office that she eventually worked in. Now, you might think that would have helped things along, but you would be wrong. The firm frowned on employees dating if they worked in the same office, and a married couple definitely could not be employed at the same location. Personal attachments were too distracting, according to management.

So, if all those events (both hers and mine) had not happened just the way they did, with just that timing, there may have been no grandchildren today! Was that due to fate, predestination, or random chance? Could we have seen that destiny in a crystal ball, tea leaves, or the stars? It was certainly not due to any scientific planning, as you can see.

So nature took its course. What does a poor guy do when he can't concentrate because he has a pretty teacher who knows more about a tough subject than he does? As it turned out, she and I shared a lot of common interests, such as outdoor sports (like skiing and hiking), beautiful music (especially when we saw Sarah Vaughan sing "Misty"), and sports events (especially the Boston Celtics). We both appreciated travel and things being well organized, and we quickly became best friends. (However, I must admit that I was a big disappointment when it came to dancing and skiing, two things she really enjoyed. I guess that proves that a perfect match in interests is not always necessary).

I suppose the stars were aligned when I proposed at Christmas time, and we spent the next fifty years learning the art of married life and being best friends. I guess that means we learned how to appreciate and accept the differences in each other, made sure that we shared all burdens as equally as possible, and put our priority on making each other happy, not just focusing on our own selfish interests.

But that is not the end of the story; it is just the beginning. Marriage also meant two lovely daughters. Having children made me realize, maybe for the first time, how much my struggling parents must have loved me. I found out that being a parent means taking a vow of poverty to afford two decades of clothing bills, children's appetites, music lessons, sports gear, hobbies, tuitions, and more. Being a parent means feeling pain, just as my parents had, from the sleepless nights when young children are sick, when they struggle with the issues of being a teen, and when they face the trials of life in a difficult society such as ours.

But those problems all fade away and are replaced by my memories of the simple joys: reading a Dr. Seuss book to wide-eyed children, holding tiny hands as they take their first steps, steadying a shaky bicycle as they find new freedom, fishing together in the evening on a quiet Adirondack Lake, and rejoicing in their success in music and sports. Those rewards are unmatched anywhere on earth.

So when I met my wife, now better known as "Grandma," it became more than a love story, it was the beginning of an adventure—an adventure that can have no end, as long as there are the joyful sounds of grandchildren.

2. MY LIST OF " HOW I MET MOTHER" EVENTS

MY LIST	READER'S LIST
Choosing the Air Force	
Electronic classes	
GI Bill for Korean vets	
Our choices of universities	
Our choice of college courses	
Available work upon graduation	
Available roommates	
Choice of employer	
A recession	
Selection of class to attend	
Matching interests	
Having children	
Music recitals/bands	
New bicycles	
Visiting Grandma/pa	
Kids' graduation day	
First grandchild	

You can add your own story in the pages at the end of the book.

3. TODAY AND TOMORROW

Today, it seems to me that both Grandmother's tea leaves and our serendipity have been partially replaced by science. Take eHarmony (the modern version of "Marryin' Sam" from the

Lil' Abner comic strip), which creates a detailed profile of each person, scientifically calculates their suitability for one another, and then introduces them for a fee. Only Marryin' Sam's mule is missing. The computer certainly broadens a person's choices beyond their normal field of vision, which more times than not was limited to fellow workers, a shared interest group, or a chance encounter at Ye Olde Tavern. Theoretically, these more scientific approaches should increase the number of "perfect marriages," but the persistently high divorce rate and trend of smaller families have not supported the theory so far.

My wife and I have been together for fifty years, through wars, recessions, career changes, tragedies, and joys. We have raised and nurtured a family, seen the world, and remained devoted to each other—all without a computer profile. However, the real test of love is not very easy to measure. That test comes when you are no longer handsome or beautiful, when the aches and the creaks make us grumpy, and patience wears thin. It is then that a little kindness, an understanding smile, and a loving touch are worth far more than they were years ago. That is a hard concept to capture in a computer.

The frosting on the cake, of course, is "grandparenting"— a job that never changes. It is the only job that provides pure joy, no responsibilities, and inspires you to be young again. Just think, I would have missed the best job of my life if I had not serendipitously met my wife!

Tomorrow, with more and more people working from home versus working in an office, plus the increasingly impersonal communications of Twitter and Facebook, the romantic work of the fates or serendipity will be even more challenged, and the dry, statistical approach of matchmakers may be more prevalent. Maybe there will be a new magazine called "Scientific Romance," or a DNA test for compatibility. Sounds boring.

Joseph Barth said, "Marriage is our last chance to grow up." Hopefully, growing up will become important again, in our kids' future.

X

RETIREMENT

Grandpa, what do you do all day?

In my retirement I go for a short swim at least once or twice every day. It's either that or buy a new golf ball."

—Gene Perret

1. IT SEEMS LIKE ONLY YESTERDAY

Retirement is a time to do all those things that you never had time for when you were working and raising kids. Of course that assumes two things: the first is that you saved your health so you could still do them, and the second is that you run out of years before you run out of money. Those are big assumptions.

In some ways, retirement is like being young again. You suddenly have time to watch the clouds go by, admire a rainbow, become an artist, learn to play the guitar, travel, or help others. You can sleep late in the morning, eat when you are hungry, and play with grandchildren as long as you want. On the other hand, if you don't have interests that keep you challenged, that you can look forward to, and that make you happy, then retirement can be a pretty frightening chapter.

Before my grandfather retired many years ago, his entire life had been wrapped up in his work, his large family, and his household chores. His only interest, if I can call it that, had been reading the newspaper each day. Once he retired, he was faced with empty days—days where Grandma would find chores for him to keep him from being underfoot. (On the other hand, she continued to be busy making quilts and clothes for grandchildren, as well as crochet and needlepoint items for her children's homes.) So, my grandpa had gone from being a boss in a high-risk job to being "bossed" (and bored to boot!), a situation that made me feel very sad for him. Of course, I use this story to justify why I play golf instead of doing chores.

My interests have changed over the years. I no longer get the same kick out of playing football as I did fifty years ago, and somehow, choosing between freezing myself on a ski lift versus sitting in the lodge drinking mulled wine seems like a no-brainer. Even more to the point, I don't even think about taking a crosscheck in hockey anymore.

However, some hobbies—music, art, and reading are just three examples—are timeless. These hobbies are a source of pleasure and, as they can never be "finished," continue to provide a sense of personal satisfaction just when you need it.

For example, Churchill spent time on his painting and writing (as well as cigars and brandy) because he said they provided an escape into a world of his own making, where the problems of the world and bodily ailments could be put aside for a while. As you get older and the aches and pains kick in, a special interest can be a wonderful diversion from thinking about your next doctor's appointment, or it can be a great companion when you are on the mend for whatever ails you (which is too frequent).

In my case, I have played golf for over fifty years. It is a game where you can play poorly and yet enjoy a walk out-doors in beautiful park-like settings, where you and your fel-low players can bond over the sadistic placement of the pins, the texture of the sand traps, or the unlucky bounce that stopped the ball from going in the cup for an ace. Or you can simply drown your sorrows in a beer together. (However, you should recall Dean Martin's advice: "If you drink, don't drive. Don't even putt.")

Some folks think golf is easy. After all, you are only trying to hit a little ball in a hole—how tough can that be? The great baseball player Hank Aaron answered that question once. He said, "It took me seventeen years to get 3,000 hits in baseball. I did it in one afternoon on the golf course." So golf is not as easy as it looks and it really does take a lot of concentra-tion, which in turn does what a retirement interest is sup-posed to do: take your mind off the problems of everyday living. As that wonderful humorist, Will Rogers, once said, "I guess there is nothing that will get your mind off everything like golf. I have never been depressed enough to take up the game, but they say you get so sore at yourself you forget to hate your enemies."

But golf is not my only retirement interest; after all, one has to have something to do at night and on rainy days. For such dire times, I enjoy bridge, a game you can play for your entire adult life, assuming you choose your partners carefully. Bridge, like golf, requires a lot of concentration, has many rules, and requires a few lucky breaks if you are to be successful at all. However, there are two large differences between bridge and golf: one is, of course, that with bridge you can sit down, indoors, without an umbrella; and the other is that in golf when you mess up no one really cares except you, while in bridge, heaven help you if you if you trump a passionate partner's ace.

If you wish to avoid stress, you could choose a simpler, gentler pastime than golf, such as fishing, painting, photography, or pinochle. To see how broad the choices really are, you can visit any Sun City location and you will see a menu of over fifty "special interest" or "activities" clubs that their residents enjoy. "Clubs" in this case are simply people with common interests—that can be anything from singing, sewing, and swimming to bocce, basketball, and badminton. The main point is that clubs (or like-minded friends) help inspire you to get away from the TV, get active, and add some zest to retirement living.

Please note that when you retire, it is very important that your wife has several interests as well. These interests will give her something besides you to focus on and significantly reduces your "to do" list. I realize this hobby may take some time away from the duties you perceive that she has at home, but believe me, it really is a good trade-off. As I said, hobbies and special interests are a very important part of a retired grandfather's life.

2. MY BUSY LIST

MY LIST	READER'S LIST
Bocce	
Bridge	
Books/ Reading	
Fishing	
Gardening	
Golf	
Harmonica	
Friendly Poker	
Scenic Hikes	
Scrabble	
Writing	
Volunteering	

3. TODAY AND TOMORROW

Today, many retirement interests are built around the computer, the Internet, and a variety of electronic devices. Genealogy, for example, is an interest that usually takes hold later in life; a switch seems to go on in our mind that says, "Whom are you descended from?" Until the switch clicked, we were too preoccupied to care; then suddenly my great uncle on my father's side is a big deal. Genealogy research once required a trip to Salt Lake City or possibly the catacombs of Ellis Island, where old microfiche of births, deaths, census, and ship passenger lists are stored. But fortunately for me, today's research is mostly done online. For example, some recent software allows long-lost relatives to combine their efforts; that way, they can share old photos and collect stories that put some life in a distant relation's lifetime. (Unfortunately, after delving back as far as the 1500s, the computer never found a relative who had left me a fortune. There must be a glitch in the software.)

In a similar vein, due to technology, you can now take bridge lessons online and actually participate in a remote game, organize a tournament, or help with scoring. But in bridge, the computer can only enhance the mechanics of the game; something like bridge is important as a social event, not just a game. Similarly, I find it a bit hard to appreciate the new electronic version of Monopoly, which has no paper money, no paper deeds to Park Place, and nobody to tease.

Fortunately, most of my favorite interests remain in familiar formats, despite new technology. Whether it is golf, fishing, or hiking, the social aspect and the physical require-ments have kept these interests pretty much the way we knew them—a comfort at my age, as I find that learning new things is harder than remembering the old ones.

The overwhelming use of technology and the forces of society have encouraged interests that are disconnected from human contact. To me, playing tennis, bowling, or golf on a Wii device really leaves a lot to be desired in terms of social-izing and involvement. But it does get the players away from daily turmoil. In addition, digital games may strengthen the family unit, if they get the family playing together. If the games achieve a goal of family bonding, technology would be making an important contribution to society.

Tomorrow will see dramatic changes in retirement. I recall that a recent magazine said that we are fast approaching a time when an eighty-year-old person is similar in health and capability to a sixty-year-old in the year 2000! I liked that idea, but that may be wishful thinking on my part. On the other hand, I saw a Maxine cartoon that said that twenty-five years from now, when today's young are old, we will have wrinkled old people whose full body tattoos are sagging and whose "golden oldies" will be rap music. That is about the scariest thought in this book!

What we do know is that people do live much longer than in eras past, and there are millions more of them. The pensions and government systems that support retirement are already strained past the breaking point, so financially I expect retirement to be less idyllic in the future. In fact, seniors will have to work many more years, just to make ends meet. Of course, that keeps husbands from being "underfoot."

Despite all the scientific advances, I can safely predict that life and retirement will always come with an expiration date. Until that date, I will continue to play bad golf, lose at poker, spoil my grandkids, join my wife in a game of Scrabble and enjoy each day as it comes along. I hope you will do the same.

FAVORITE PLACES

Grandpa, what is your favorite place in the whole world?

"My favorite place to be is wherever you are."

—Pooh

1. IT SEEMS LIKE ONLY YESTERDAY

When my great- grandparents made the difficult move to the North America in the 1700s, they could not believe the abundance of food; the clean, safe water and fresh air; the citizen-oriented government; the ability to travel freely; and the wide, open, tree-filled spaces. Here, they could aspire to have their own home and yard, or even a farm, and not live in poorly cared-for rental flats that lacked heat, running water, and sewage, as they had in the old country. They often said that they felt they had found heaven. So if you asked them about their favorite place, the answer was always the same, America".

In their era (the 1920s and '30s) our children would be shocked to know that there were no McDonald's. There were no motels to speak of, no rental cars, and Disneyland was a future dream. It was really a time when most folks stayed at home, and home was their favorite place.

However, two hundred years later, American men and women, like my father and uncles, got a new perspective on travel when they unexpectedly got sent to Rome, London, Honolulu, Tokyo, or the jungles of places like New Guinea. There was a hit song written earlier that said it all: "How 'ya gonna keep 'em down on the farm after they've seen Paree?" Even if you did not travel to exotic places at Uncle Sam's expense, all the latest movies, plus the well-embellished stories of returning veterans, made travel so glamorous that everybody seemed ready to set sail for some magical spot.

After the war, international business travel boomed. In addition, vacationers began their search for a Shangri-La. It was a new type of freedom, a luxury once reserved for the rich, which grew into a $700 billion industry. Interestingly, though, no matter who the traveler was or where they went, the returning traveler with the alluring stories of far-off places were the same ones who almost daily talked about how much they wanted to get back to their favorite place—home. I guess for business and military travelers, Alice said it best during her adventures in Wonderland: "It was much pleasanter at home, when one wasn't always growing larger and smaller, and being ordered about by mice and rabbits." A timeless comment, I think.

I never really knew what the phrase "home is where the heart is" meant until I was traveling a lot and, suddenly, at the end of two weeks, no matter where I was or how exciting things were, a switch seemed to click and I would be ready—almost desperate—to go home. When I arrived home to a familiar bed, daily routine, loving family, and well-worn friends, the world seemed more comfortable and more complete. So I must confess that despite over a million miles of airline travel, "home" is still my favorite place to be.

By the way, that does not mean you shouldn't travel. Quite the contrary, grandkids should certainly travel because the experience really helps a person understand not only other people in faraway lands, but also helps provide perspective on things at home, something we all need in this complex world. For example, when I traveled through Burma (Myanmar) and Nepal, I enjoyed the rustic transportation, old flush toilets, lack of heating and running water and air-conditioning, and the unique food, but it also made me appreciate the many things we take for granted at home and why my grandparents said that living in the United States is being close to heaven.

When I traveled in Kenya, every day was a new thrill, whether we were learning about the culture or absorbed by the world of wildlife. One night a tribe of baboons surrounded our tent because we had inadvertently left some food open after a snack, and the guides had to drive away the invaders with warning shots. We also encountered a bear in Yellowstone, a moose on a golf course in Banff, and an avalanche in Switzerland—each a wonderful adventure that contributed to making life a joy. But after a while, we always longed for home.

I learned that each place has its own character, one that sets it apart from the others, and makes any comparison or choice of a favorite very difficult. The Himalayas and the Alps both have breathtaking mountain vistas, but you can't compare the two, as the people and cultures in each location are so unique. Similarly, when you travel in Ireland, the the free spirit and irrepressible humor of the people makes for a delightful trip, while a short trip to England offers a wonderful environment of history and pageantry. Here are two islands that are adjacent, yet not comparable in culture. Even a trip to the islands of Hawaii, with its wonderful beaches and balmy air defies comparison to the lovely islands of New Zealand; one is aimed at laid-back tourism and the other at a blend of farming, fishing, and outdoor adventure. There is so much to see if you look behind the scenery and see the cultures. that each place is a new experience.

I happen to enjoy things that are well organized and dependable; I always felt that life is too short to waste looking for missing things or waiting in lines. If you have that personality, then Japan is one of the best places to visit. Everything works as it is supposed to, everything runs on time, people are always courteous and take responsibility for their actions, and even the food you buy is perfectly presented. I recall the subway stop in Shinjuku, a commuting hub for more than 3 million people each day, yet the trains were always on time, the crowds were very orderly, and the trash and graffiti were almost nonexistent. Even so, I enjoyed the mountains and fishing villages even more, as they retained the traditions of old Japan and were steeped in history. Certainly, the Japanese culture, scenery, and people made it one of my favorite places.

My very favorite summer place is a lake in the Adirondacks, a rustic spot that was perfect for canoeing, fishing and hiking. There is nothing so peaceful as the rumbling clouds and hammering rain of an Adirondack summer thunderstorm, or the early morning lake that is so clear that it acts like a mirror to the sky. The soft breezes, laughing children, and wood smoke in the air make all the hustle and bustle of our lives seem a bit silly. That is why my wife went there as a child, why my children went there every year until high school, and why we go back whenever we can. After my thousands of miles of travels around the world, an Adirondack lake is still my favorite summer getaway.

2. MY FAVORITE PLACES

MY LIST	READER'S LIST
Home	
Swiss Alps	
Hawaii	
New Zealand	
Ireland	
Paris	
Mount Fuji/ Japan	
Yosemite	
Yellowstone	
Upstate New York lakes	
Monterey and Carmel, California	
Pinehurst, North Carolina	
Banff, Canada	
Williamsburg, Virginia	

3. TODAY AND TOMORROW

Today, the world is set up for travelers. Travel is fast, clean (usually), dependable, and affordable—all the things it was not when we were young. Trains no longer puff plumes of smoke and send soot in through open windows; planes rarely take elevator-like, stomach-churning drops through air pockets; ships handle most seas with ease and have become small floating cities; and potholed roads have given way to smooth highways, traveled by automobiles with built-in travel guides and better upholstery than we have in our homes.

Better yet, we have the time to travel. Today most people have ample vacation weeks and weekends, have many affordable offers from competing travel companies, and can get more out of a trip through the magic of Internet research.

So, as Mark Twain said, "Twenty years from now you will be more disappointed by the things that you didn't do than by the ones you did do. So throw off the bowlines. Sail away from the safe harbor. Catch the trade winds in your sails. Explore. Dream. Discover." If your grandchildren follow his advice, they will also value "home" even more.

Tomorrow may be more limited in travel for a while, simply due to the danger that lurks in so many locales around the world. For example, the Somali pirates have brought back the fear from the days of the old Barbary pirates, and Mexico now makes the old West look safe. Hopefully, we are in an era of one step back and two steps forward.

I suspect, in our grandchildren's time, that the space travel adventures of *Buck Rogers in the 25*[th] *Century*, which was written in the 1920s, as well as the newer *Star Trek* stories, will gradually become a reality. During that period, new methods of high-speed travel will make today's aircraft and ships seem like a slow-motion movie. These new methods of travel, along with satellite communications will make every place on our planet accessible to travelers.

Despite all those advancements, I predict that for most folks, "home" will still be the favorite destination in the universe. Someone once said that the best part of adventure is the part that brings you home. That may never change.

GREEN

Grandpa, why wasn't your generation "green"?

"Progress might have been alright once, but it went on too long."

—Ogden Nash

1. IT SEEMS LIKE ONLY YESTERDAY

Change usually sneaks up on us. Suddenly, ninja-like, it appears, "whops" us on the side of the head, and makes us wonder: When did that change? How did I not notice this was happening? Who was stacking the deck? How come nobody told me about this?

Today, for example, our country has roughly three times more people living here than when I grew up. We had seven times more folks who lived on farms back then—roughly twenty percent of the population lived on farms, versus three percent today. All those people mean that in two generations we tripled the demand for water, fuel, electricity, roads, cars, trash, parking spots, and service jobs and yet we <u>reduced</u> homegrown food—all gradual changes, invisible changes, that we now realize are "whopping" us pretty hard.

When I was young, we were "green," but did not know it! However, being green is a lot easier when you don't have any green (money, that is). For example, my mother insisted that we turn off the lights when we left a room, keep the house temperature at sixty-five degrees in the winter, and never leave the water running. (She relented on the use of water once a week, Saturday night, our weekly bath time, which was a mandatory preparation for church.) Mother was not applying for green sainthood; her frugality was driven by the cost of these "luxuries." The need to wear a sweater in the house or to sleep under a goose-down quilt were minor inconveniences to meet her credo of "waste not, want not," a slogan that dictated the lifestyle of most Depression-influenced people.

Some other big "green" differences, at least until the late 1950s, are pretty startling. For example, very few homes had air-conditioning, and home heating was via steam or hot water radiators. Most homes burned non-green coal, wood, or kerosene—fuels you could see and realize how much you

were using, which meant that every shovel of coal was literally money in the furnace. Consequently, heat was grudgingly
used. (This same syndrome was evident when the credit card
replaced cash. People are more frugal when they actually can
see cash disappearing.)

Likewise, most suburban and city dwellers (including my
grandparents) did not own automobiles, and if they did, it
was one car per family. Suburban and city folks used public transport, bicycled, or (heaven forbid) walked. And, by
the way, there were few planes, almost no refrigerated trucks,
and certainly no sixteen-wheeler, gas-guzzling trucks on the
roads. For example, the 1954 Nash Metro and Volkswagen
Beetle got nearly 40 mpg at a time when gas was twenty-one
cents per gallon. That was before Detroit chose to focus on
fancy features and fuel efficiency lost out.

One of the biggest "green" changes since I was young is
the use of plastics. This was foretold, as you may recall, in the
1967 movie, *The Graduate*, when Mr. Benjamin said about the
future, "I want you to remember one word, just one word:
plastics." Up to that point, our milk and all drinks were delivered in bottles, most of which were returned and reused. All
glass was made of simple, available sand. Our vegetables and
meat products were wrapped or covered by wax paper, not
plastic, and prepared foods were found in cans of all sizes. We
had no plastic boxes, trays, or plastic-covered frozen foods.
Grocery bags were made of paper; water pipes were all made
of copper or steel, and we drank water from the tap (or if
Mother wasn't looking, from the rubber garden hose).

We were so green, that the only thing in our home that
had a battery was my electric train set, which had a big "C"
battery. There were no portable radios, phones, TV remotes,
portable power tools, or battery-operated kitchen appliances.
There were no batteries anywhere, except our car. How
"green" was that?

However, all was not perfect. We did have lead-based paint, and we also used too much paper, putting a strain on our forests. Coal- and wood-burning furnaces polluted the air, smoke stacks of steel plants and chemical factories spewed more pollutants, coal mines endangered lives and local water supplies, and pesticides were widely used and toxic. However, the scale of these problems was far, far less than the same practices would be today, due to the smaller population and more frugal attitude.

Before the war, we had used kerosene, an inefficient shale oil, in our stoves. The discovery of high-grade oil in the mid-east allowed Britain to convert her war ships from coal to oil, a change that increased her ships' range and speed. Oil eventually became the fundamental fuel and technology of the boom years in the U.S. and Europe. And then, further wartime ingenuity opened the Pandora's box of nuclear power.

The other big changes in "greenness" were driven by the technical innovations and societal attitudes inherited from WWII, innovations such as higher-speed trains; larger, more powerful commercial aircraft; microwave ovens; refrigerated transportation; packaged meals; the miniaturization of technology; and even the miracle of rental cars. Trips that had taken our grandparents months took our parents weeks, and then took us only hours. But this dramatically increased the consumption of our resources, increased costs of maintenance, and added to the pollution of the air and water. How much they added is a daily argument.

In addition, some lifestyle changes were fostered by the harsh realities of the war years, and other changes were wrought by science and then carried to extremes. The war had fostered a new mobility and promoted a sense of "taking care of me and mine," then advertising compounded this culture, fostering people's desire for "stuff"—sometimes referred to as "keeping up with the Joneses."

"We the people" simply did not see the collective side effects of so many people acquiring so many goods. It was something akin to too many cows grazing in a field until they all starve to death—a common-sense issue, but one where only science, industry, or government could have had the perspective to see that the rapids that we were riding would eventually lead to a dangerous waterfall. But asking industry for their perspective is like expecting the fox to act as a guard for the henhouse. So the issues of waste, water, pollution, and toxicity are now "hitting us on the head." Sorry about that.

2. MY LIST OF CHANGES AFFECTING "GREEN"

MY LIST	READER'S LIST
Population doubled	
Air travel (domestic, international)	
Battery-driven devices (cell phone)	
Foods (frozen, fast food)	
Number and size of automobiles	
Refrigerated trucks/ trains	
WWII inventions (microwave)	
Mobile society	
Housing boom	
Plastic packaging (bags, wrap)	
Keeping up with the Joneses	
Preservatives (toxins)	
Responsibility (personal, corporate)	
Loss of public transit	

3. TODAY AND TOMORROW

Art Buchwald said, some forty years ago,

> *And Man created the plastic bag and the tin and alumi-num can and the cellophane wrapper and the paper plate, and this was good because Man could then take his automo-bile and buy all his food in one place and He could save that which was good to eat in the refrigerator and throw away that which had no further use. And soon the earth was covered with plastic bags and aluminum cans and paper plates and disposable bottles and there was nowhere to sit down or walk, and Man shook his head and cried: "Look at this God-awful mess."*

No, I am not suggesting that we reject all the advances we've made. Many changes are real boons to mankind, and in fairness, we could not have coped with the big population growth without some equally big changes in how we made things. However, many changes have had unforeseen or unheeded side effects. Below, I have outlined some of these changes, their impacts, and hopefully things that our grandchildren will improve.

Changes and Side Effects

We grow more food, but it has less nutrition.

We make food last longer, but have added questionable chemicals.

We have made great advances in batteries, but not in their toxicity.

We have disposable plastic bottles and packaging, but they fill our oceans.

We take more medicines and yet we are less healthy and spend more on healthcare.

We live longer, but less wisely.

In two generations, we have seen more scientific and materialistic progress than in all the years of history before us. That may be great, but the goal we embarked on was to make the earth and our country a better place to live, to make mankind freer, smarter, stronger, and healthier for the generations yet to come. If we do not meet those goals, then I think the price of progress has been too high. There is a Native American proverb that is fitting: "We do not inherit the earth from our ancestors. We borrow it from our children." We have, I fear, borrowed too heavily.

For **tomorrow,** science will continue to bring changes that extend our lives, provide access to even more knowledge, allow us to travel faster and further, and offer new approaches to nutrition. But who will make sure we have a sustainable future? Who will create a better legacy for our children than our current self-destructive habits? Will our children and grandchildren get "whopped on the head" and wake up to a world managed by the proverbial mad scientists, mad bankers, intelligent robots, or even worse, a world devoid of natural resources? Maybe our grandchildren will follow the Superman script, where he leaves his planet, Krypton, and comes to Metropolis because his planet is no longer habitable. Or maybe, in a more positive vein, an H.G. Wells space traveler will come back, threaten us, and offer some alternatives, hoping to bring us to our senses.

I have faith, however, that our grandchildren will grab control and use all our progress to build a better world. They can start with just three words: "No more plastic."

Thanks for the Memories

What the heart has once known, it shall never forget.

—Author unknown

I hope these few stories and examples have stirred up hundreds of your old memories. I hope I inspired smiles, laughs, and even a few tears along the way. Your life has been an incredible journey, filled with special people, special events, and special moments, many of which will never be experienced by future generations.

Maybe you found, hidden in a corner of your mind, an old jukebox of songs you can still hum along with. Perhaps there was an old photo album there as well, with vivid memories of old cars, old homes, and old friends, as well as memories of sadness, a few mistakes, and many trials. You might also recall the incredible people and events that made life so special.

Recall the special people who set the examples we hoped to follow, giants in their own way. We had the incomparable determination of Knute Rockne at Notre Dame and Lou Gehrig of the Yankees. There was the wonderful dreamer Walt Disney, the genius of Albert Einstein and the leadership of "Ike." There were standards of courage set by FDR, Churchill, Bill Maudlin, and our servicemen everywhere. These public figures, as well as some of our own personal acquaintances, made us know we could be better than we were and inspired us to try harder.

Then there were the entertainers who made our journey so special: Bing Crosby, Mario Lanza, Howard Keel, Nat King Cole, Elvis, Patsy Kline, Katherine Grayson, and so many others. Stop for a moment and hear their voices in your head and the great feelings they generated. Of course, dancing to the big band sounds of Jimmy Dorsey, Benny Goodman, and Duke Ellington will never be topped, in my opinion.

Then there were the folks who made you laugh at the world and yourself, people who put our life in perspective. We were blessed with laughter from true comedians, ranging from Dick Van Dyke to Mel Blanc to Tim Conway and the buttoned-down mind of Bob Newhart, as well as the roll-in-the-aisle humor of Jackie Gleason, Red Skelton, Bob Hope, and Danny Kaye. And one of the best, as you may recall, was the genius of Steve Allen.

We also enjoyed the pioneer days of the miracle of television, especially family television that, blessedly, had very few commercials. My all-time favorite was *Laugh-In*. A few younger shows were *The Cisco Kid and his friend Pancho, Lassie*, and *Bonanza*, which eventually gave way as we grew older to *F-Troop, Death Valley Days, Gilligan's Island, The Man from Uncle, Dragnet,* The *Carol Burnett* Show, *Candid Camera*, and *The Perry Como Show*.

Movie characters, in those golden days, usually portrayed values and virtues, so the stars became more than just actors; many of them influenced our ideals. Jimmy Cagney, who played both comic and street-tough with equal ease, usually showed why bad guys lost. Humphrey Bogart and Edward G. Robinson showed why good looks weren't everything. Charles Laughton, Sidney Greenstreet, and Basil Rathbone were typecast in wonderful dramatic roles, as was Joan Crawford. Of course, we had strong character examples set by John Wayne and Gregory Peck, and my favorite actor, Spencer Tracey. What a cast!

It is amazing to think of how fortunate we were to have all these people and their creativity setting the tone and tenor of our golden years.

Scientific progress in our lifetime was also mind-boggling, to say the least. And yet, when reading this book's "Today" sections, you might have thought of the classic Charles Dickens line that begins, "It was the best of times, it was the worst of times, it was the age of wisdom, it was the age of foolishness." To which our era might add, "it was an age of unimaginable and somewhat unmanageable scientific progress."

The list of inventions goes on and on, including (vitally) the many inventions making it possible to write a book like this one without ink ribbons, carbon paper, or even Wite-Out. By many measures, scientific progress has certainly made our grandkids lives' much easier than ours.

The speed of change however, has made some of us feel obsolete or old-fashioned, as our kids will remind us. However, just recall that all today's gizmos will soon be in a wristwatch or earring, just like Dick Tracey foretold back in 1930. In addition, our grandkids will colonize Mars, just as Buck Rogers foretold in 1928, or live under the sea as Jules Verne wrote almost one hundred and fifty years ago. It may also make you feel better to know that science will never replace a hot fudge sundae. Progress cannot improve perfection.

If you still think the coming technical changes that I mentioned in my "Tomorrow" sections are just conjecture, I would ask you to think back. How have you done lately in finding paper for your technically advanced Polaroid camera? Do your CDs work well in your miraculous Sony Walkman? And isn't that technical "marvel" up in the attic a Princess telephone? You know, the one right next to the rabbit ear antennas? Oh, does that once-amazing floppy disk in the desk drawer have any important stuff on it? Change, as we all learned, is something you can count on; it is relentless.

Science may have improved many aspects of life, but when it comes to lifestyle progress, I think that my stories and the reader's memories have shown that we missed the boat. We forgot that, in addition to inventing clever devices, we were also supposed to pass on the human lessons, the understanding of what is really important, lessons that each new generation must build upon or painfully relearn. We got so caught up with progress, we forgot that a successful society is totally dependent on human virtues, and that scientific improvements are not the end objective of life. Living wisely is the goal. We forgot to explain that being an honorable person, being dependable, being a friend in time of need, and earning family love are the real treasures, ones that can't be purchased at any price. We now know what is really important, but as our imaginary grandchild asked in this book's opening paragraph: "How come you never told me this stuff?"

Some of the virtues that we learned, either through teaching or tough mistakes, and which many of my examples have touched upon, were self-reliance, integrity, dependability, compassion, ambition, thrift, common sense, and, of course, the golden rule. That is not to say that we were perfect followers of those precepts; we were not. But the old-fashioned proximity of relatives, the long-term relationship with neighbors, the strict teachers, religious beliefs, stay-at-home mothers, and belts of our fathers offered us the persuasive constraints and direction that helped most of us try to meet those ideals.

Sadly, in today's more complex world, a time when role models would be very beneficial, most of those wholesome guideline providers are gone. There are few neighborhoods, as we knew them. Discipline at home and school has been curtailed for many reasons. Stay-at-home moms are pretty rare. And there are far more bad public role models than good ones. A pessimistic old-timer once wrote this obituary:

Today we mourn the passing of a beloved old friend, **Common Sense.** He will be remembered as having cultivated such valuable lessons as:
- Knowing when to come in out of the rain;
- Why the early bird gets the worm;
- Life isn't always fair;
- A penny saved is a penny earned
- and maybe it was my fault.

Of course, we now know what we wished we had known back then. But, as you know, very few people take common-sense," how-to-live" advice very well. Somehow kids feel that taking advice minimizes them. That is why the real stories about your life, ones that provide an example of "lessons learned," have a much better chance of being retained than any lecture on that subject. (By the way, when a grandchild says, "Grandpa, I already heard that story," it should make you feel great, not bad. It means they really heard your story the first time and it stuck!)

Storytellers have been an important influence on society throughout all history. Some famous storytellers are Hans Christian Anderson, Aesop, Mark Twain, and Dr. Seuss. But the stories that really influence a life are personal ones; stories that are passed down through the generations, from family member to family member. These are the most useful stories, ones that define how to live day by day. This is about handling success and failure, love and disappointments, harm and healing. It is about handling those feelings when you drop your ice cream cone, lose a friend, or win a game. Sharing personal stories separates the "fads of living" from the practical "reality of living." These are the stories that come from the individual moments, the joys, the mistakes and the sorrows. Ones that are based on a lifetime library of practical knowledge and ones that teach common sense. The stories of our lives, those fleeting moments in time, have shaped our own values and, if shared, can add strength to our family's future.

Our grandchildren will face many challenges—major wars, strong international competition, new advances in space travel, several recessions or depressions, high inflation, shortages of food and water, longer lives, and possibly less freedom. Will our grandchildren's collective "life skills" help them cope with all those changes? If they are to survive they need to focus not just on science, but also on the virtues that make people strong, the ageless human skills that can nurture common sense and deal with the challenges of living. Will they recall your stories? Will they be up to the task?

As I looked back at the sections of the book regarding the Good Old Days, Today and Tomorrow, it made me more optimistic that our grandchildren will stand tall and overcome tomorrow's challenges, because their challenges are not so different from the ones that you, I, and our parents faced and overcame in our lifetimes. The details may differ, but the challenges of wars, recessions, shortages, failures, and successes remain the same. Common sense still determines life's outcome, creativity still helps us leap tall buildings, and the strength that comes from family and friends is still the foundation, the shoulders we stand on, to reach greater heights. They, too, shall overcome.

"The history of our grandparents is remembered not with rose petals but in the laughter and tears of their children and their children's children. It is into us that the lives of grandparents have gone. It is in us that their history leads us to the future."

—Morse

Appendix

I. My Favorite websites
- Childhood

Old Time Radio Classics-	http://www.archive.org/details/oldtimeradio
Early TV and Radio-	http://backwhen.com/EarlyTV.html
Old Toys Archive-	http://www.thepeoplehistory.com/toys.html
Best Ever Kids Books-	http://childrensbooksguide.com/top-100
Old Westerns Archive-	http://www.ropeandwire.com/MainPages/Movies.html
Sears Catalogs from the Forties-	http://www.wishbookweb.com/
Elementary School Memories-	http://backwhen.com/ElementarySchool1900s.html

- Growing Pains

The Fifties and Music-	http://oldfortyfives.com/TakeMeBackToTheFifties.htm
Videos of the '50s-	http://backwhen.com/1950sVideo.htm
Baseball of the '50s (and beyond)-	http://baseballsgreatesthitters.com/ERA_4_-_1950-1964.html
100 Best Movies-	www.afi.com/100years/movies.aspx

-Grown Up

Cars of the '50s and '60s-	http://backwhen.com/CarsMadeInTheUSA.html
Girls We Loved-	http://backwhen.com/WomenIRemember.html
Family Life Photo Gems-	http://backwhen.com/FamilyLife.htm
Military Photo Gems-	http://backwhen.com/UncleSam1900s.htm
The Pill Changed Life-	http://www.pbs.org/wgbh/amex/pill/peopleevents/p_mrs.html
Art Linkletter/Kids-	http://www.youtube.com/watch?v=_UgLpRvX7Qk&feature=related

-Doing Your Own Book

Learn how to do your own book, add to this one or request seminars at your location, go to: http://www.backwhen.com

Acknowledgments

This book has been over seventy years in the making; so forgive me if I do not acknowledge all the folks that helped shape this book. Please charge it to my poor memory and not a lack of appreciation. My biggest thanks go to my family, for their suggestions, as well as their patience with me while I was lost in thought, retrieving memories, or grumpily editing the book for the "umpteenth" time. The book is also the result of the friendship, inspiration and suggestions of my long-time business partner, Bill Barley.

The many people who attended my Memories Seminars were a great encouragement to me, as were the friends who read the early drafts of my ramblings. They kindly reminded me when I forgot things or kicked me when my recollections were too optimistic or too jaded; something most writers seem to need. Even better, when they corroborated my memories, they convinced me that I was not the only crazy guy in the room.

Terry Armstrong Graphics, (armstronggraphics.com) did the illustrations in the book as well as the e-book illustrations. Mary Helen Fein, at Parallax Design Group (maryhelen@ parallaxdesigngroup), created our Backwhen website, which supports this book. I have worked with both Terry and Mary Helen for the past decade and I am constantly amazed at their creativity, dependability and can-do attitudes. They are a joy to work with.

This book is my reward, in a way, for spending decades in the computer field. The computer I have today, a Mac with

MS Word, is the only reason I could get the job done. Writing this book with an old typewriter and carbon paper and without the ability to relocate sentences, paragraphs, and entire sections would have taken me years and interrupted so many golf games that I doubt I would have ever finished. Checking my facts via Google as I typed, rather than spending days at the library, also added to my enjoyment. For all this, I must thank IBM, Bill Gates, and Steve Jobs for their efforts in making this book possible.

Finally, I have to thank my parents for having the foresight to have me during the "Golden Years" of our country, and then instilling in me at least a few of the virtues that helped me enjoy the wonderful opportunities that made my life so special.

Thank you, one and all.

About the Author

Old Bill, the author, having lived seven decades, has a broad beam, both anatomically and in terms of life experience. Over the years he has lived on both coasts of the U.S. and in the heartland, enjoying both small town life and the bustle of large cities. He has spent half his time working for large firms and half in small business. He has also had multiple stints working and studying abroad, all of which added to his curmudgeonly view of all types of cultures, organizations, and politics.

More recently, after he spent forty years working on projects using advanced technologies in the computer industry, he spent the past decade researching and lecturing on the people and events that are the legacies of the past two senior generations in the U.S. So in a way Old Bill has had one foot in the future and one in the past—a split personality, so to speak—which gives him a cockeyed view of where we have been and where we might be going.

He enjoys reading, but has found that interspersing a Zane Grey western with a tome on technology or some Pogo strips with a history of WWII gives him a better perspective on what he reads. His musicical idols, which ranges from Eddie Arnold to Mario Lanza, and his movie idols, including John Wayne, Yul Brynner and Rex Harrison, are equally eclectic, revealing that either Old Bill has boundless interests or has a totally disorganized mind.

The "Grandpa, Were You Young Once?" project started quite simply, nearly five years ago. It was born of the desire to give some of Old Bill's success back to the community. The original idea was to help seniors get more use out of computers by helping them create "memory books." In the course of the lectures and online correspondences, he was impressed by the uniqueness of each senior's life. In one class he had an RAF fighter pilot from WWII who had never talked about his experiences. In another he had a retired principal from one of the toughest schools in California. But the most interesting might have been a retired cleaning woman who had put three kids through college.

Each person had unique memories to talk about: the personal joys, heartbreaks, people, challenges, and successes of daily life, an archive of memories that a history book barely touches. These memories were unforgettable moments in their lives.

However, most seniors think they have forgotten all those details, and if they do remember they find it hard to express them in an interesting way. So Old Bill introduced a simple concept called "key word association" in his lectures. If he said "first grade" then each member of the audience would offer a memory from that era. Each time they did, they triggered a new memory from another member of the audience. Soon the class just bubbled with pleasure as the memories flooded back. One attendee came up to Old Bill the day after a class and said he was mad because he could not get to sleep the night before; he kept remembering things he hadn't thought about in decades.

From Old Bill's seminar series came this book, the third book the author has written and surely the one that will bring the most pleasure; of course, that is an easy guess, as both prior books were textbooks having to do with business management.

The author has several degrees to his credit, but feels that this project has taught him more about "how progress happens" and "how to live in spite of it" than anything taught in a university. By sharing his own memories, the author relearned quite a few lessons, recalled important people who had helped shape his life, thought about some mistakes he made along the way, and better understood his own value system. The results made him even more determined to help seniors pass on their memories to the younger generations.

Which leads us to Old Bill's big question: "How do our grandchildren learn the practical facts of life, when the world seems to want folks to be impractical?" That is a driving question behind his book and seminars. The book, including the reader's notes, helps seniors recall and enjoy the past, with the hope that seniors will pass along their lessons of a lifetime in an easy-to-read format that helps young folks avoid learning the hard way.

While none of us can forecast the future, we do know who will be running things. Today they are called "my grandchildren;" tomorrow they will be "the persons in charge." Old Bill is convinced that they need good examples of how to live and need them now; they need your shoulders to stand on, so tomorrow they can more easily reach the stars.

Notes

Notes

12918936R00135

Made in the USA
Charleston, SC
06 June 2012